THE LITTLE OFFICE OF THE HOLY FACE

SENSUS FIDELIUM PRESS

Charlotte, North Carolina

ISBN: 978-1-966961-02-4

For more information, please visit sensusfideliumpress.com

TRUE IMAGE OF THE SACRED COUNTENANCE
OF OUR LORD JESUS CHRIST
Preserved and Venerated in the Basilica,of St. Peter, in the
Vatican, Rome

The Little Office of the Holy Face

A Manual of Devotion and Reparation
TO THE
Holy Face of Our Lord and Savior Jesus Christ
From approved and original sources
by the
Sisters of the Divine Compassion
"By *those thorns which opened each a fountain of life, have mercy on those whose unbelief and pride of opinion crown Thee anew* "

CONTENTS

SUNDAY

MATINS

Hail Mary.

O Jesus, Thou hast promised all good gifts to those who adore Thy Holy Face in reparation for blasphemies uttered against Thy holy Name and the teachings of Thy Church. Offer to the eternal Father, we implore Thee, these prayers which we pour forth for the greater glory of God and the conversion of sinners.

Our Father who art in heaven, look not upon us only, but upon the Face of Thy Christ.

Versicle. O Lord, show us Thy Face and we shall be saved.

Responsory. Turn Thy Face towards us and give us peace.

V. His mighty Name shall be our shield.

R. And His adorable Face shall be our fortress.

Glory be to the Father, and to the Son,

and to the Holy Ghost, as it was in the beginning,

is now, and ever shall be, world without end. Amen.

Hymn

Jesus, the very thought of Thee

With sweetness fills my breast,

But sweeter far Thy Face to see,

And in Thy presence rest.

No voice can sing, no heart can frame,

Nor can the memory find

A sweeter sound than Jesu's Name,

The Saviour of mankind,

St. Bernard

O Lord, I will sing Thy praise in the sanctuary, I will kneel before the tabernacle where Thou dost dwell for love of me. I will receive the King of my soul with a humble and grateful heart.

I consecrate to Thee every hour of this day. Thou hast given me a work to do. Thou hast made me that I might know Thee and love Thee and serve Thee here, and be happy with Thee for all eternity. Let me not fail of the end for which Thou hast created me.

Thou hast said, Remember to keep holy the Sabbath-day. Thou hast commanded us to rest, and I will take my rest in Thee.

Antiphon. "THE WORLD IS FULL OF SIN. THE NAME OF GOD IS BLASPHEMED, AND BY PROFANATION OF

THE SABBATH THEY HAVE FILLED UP THE MEASURE OF THEIR INIQUITY."[1]

We invoke Thee, O holy Name of the living God, by the lips of Jesus in the Blessed Sacrament; and in reparation for the blasphemies by which that Name is profaned, we offer Thee, O most patient Lord, by the hands of Thy gentle Mother, the sacred Hosts reposing in our tabernacles.

V. The Name of the Lord is mighty and greatly to be praised.

R. Come and adore it.

Let us Pray

Eternal Father, I offer Thee the Holy Face of Our Lord. May it appease Thy just anger. Remember how it was crowned with thorns for our sins, and how it set itself as a rock to meet and break the waves of Thy justice, that we might be spared.

Look upon the wounds of Jesus. Unceasingly they plead for mercy—for mercy on those who have rebelled against Thee.

V. O most sweet Face of Jesus, have compassion on our misery.

R. Mother most loving, plead for us with Jesus; convert us, and save us.

St. Michael, pray for us.

St. Veronica, pray for us.

May the souls of the faithful departed through the mercy of God rest in peace. Amen.

---

1. The words in small capitals are those spoken by our Lord to Sister Marie de St. Pierre.

Sunday

Lauds

V. His mighty Name shall be our shield.

R. And His adorable Face shall be our fortress.

Glory be to the Father.

Hymn

O Jesus, Jesus, dearest Lord,

Forgive me if I say,

For very love, Thy sacred Name

A thousand times a day.

I love Thee so I know not how

My transports to control:

Thy love is like a burning fire,

Within my very soul.

St. Bernard

Come, let us adore the Name of the Lord, let us prostrate ourselves before Him.

In union with the saints in heaven and the just on earth, in union with the whole Church and in the name of all creatures, let us praise the mighty Name at which hell trembles and the court of heaven rejoices.

Blessed be the Name of Jesus. It is the golden key which opens the treasures of the divine mercy. It is the rallying cry of the angelic hosts. It is the standard of victory in our conflict with the powers of darkness. At this sacred Name the adversary of souls is put to flight and the heart of God overflows with divine compassion.

O blessed Name, be ever my strength, my glory, and my love.

Ant. THE VIOLATION OF THE FIRST THREE COMMANDMENTS HAS AROUSED THE FATHER'S IRE. THE HOLY NAME OF GOD BLESPHEMED AND THE SEVENTH DAY PROFANED HAVE FILLED UP THE MEASURE OF INIQUITY.

V. THESE SINS HAVE MOUNTED TO THE ETERNAL THRONE, AND PROVOKED THE WRATH OF GOD.

R. In six days the Lord made heaven and earth, the sea, and all things that are in them, and rested on the seventh day: therefore the Lord blessed the seventh day, and sanctified it.[1]

---

1. Exodus xx. 11.

V. The Name of God is mighty and greatly to be praised.

R. Come and adore it.

Let us pray.

Eternal Father, I offer Thee the Holy Face of Our Lord. May it appease Thy just anger. Remember how it was crowned with thorns for our sins, and how it set itself as a rock to meet and break the waves of Thy justice, that we might be spared.

Look upon the wounds of Jesus. Unceasingly they plead for mercy—-for mercy on those who have rebelled against Thee.

V. O most sweet Face of Jesus, have compassion on our misery.

R. Mother most loving, plead for us with Jesus; convert us, and save us.

St. Michael, pray for us.

St. Veronica, pray for us.

May the souls of the faithful departed through the mercy of God rest in peace. Amen.

Sunday

Prime

V. His mighty Name shall be our shield.

R. And His adorable Face shall be our fortress.

Hymn

O wonderful, that Thou shouldst let

So vile a heart as mine

Love Thee with such a love as this,

And make so free with Thine!

For Thou to me art all in all

My honor and my wealth,

My heart's desire, my body's strength,

My soul's enduring health.

St. Bernard

My God, what have I to offer Thee but a life spent in displeasing Thee? How have I received Thy sacraments? Where is my obedience to the law of God? The things of this world have absorbed my heart, and often God was not in my thoughts.

Thou hast pursued me with Thy mercies, and I have flown from Thee, my Friend and my Father.

When Thou hast chastised me, I have fallen at Thy feet and promised fidelity; but alas! when Thy Face was softened towards me, I have forgotten my repentance and my promises and have offended Thee anew. I confess that I am unworthy of the least of Thy graces. O Thou who hast redeemed me and drawn me from my sins, anchor my faithless heart in Thine. Yet once again, show me Thy compassionate Face and teach me to pray.

Ant. "THEY HAVE KINDLED MY WRATH BECAUSE THEY PROFANED MY HOLY DAY."

V. "I SEEK FOR SOULS WHO WILL MAKE REPARATION."

R. "The Lord spoke to Moses, saying: Speak to the children of Israel, and thou shalt say to them: See that thou keep My Sabbath, because it is a sign between Me and you in your generations, that you may know that I am the Lord who sanctifies you. This is an everlasting covenant between Me and the children of Israel, a perpetual sign."

V. The Name of the Lord is mighty, and greatly to be praised.

R. Come and adore it.

Let us pray.

Eternal Father, I offer Thee the Holy Face of Our Lord. May it appease Thy just anger. Remember how it was crowned with thorns

for our sins, and how it set itself as a rock to meet and break the waves of Thy justice, that we might be spared.

Look upon the wounds of Jesus. Unceasingly they plead for mercy—-for mercy on those who have rebelled against Thee.

V. O most sweet Face of Jesus, have compassion on our misery.

R. Mother most loving, plead for us with Jesus; convert us, and save us.

St. Michael, pray for us.

St. Veronica, pray for us.

May the souls of the faithful departed through the mercy of God rest in peace. Amen.

SUNDAY

TIERCE

V. His mighty Name shall be our shield.

R. And His adorable Face shall be our fortress.

Glory be to the Father.

Hymn

The glory of thy Face enlightens me;

My risen Jesus, bring me safe to Thee;

Free me, Thou dearest God, from all but Thee;

Break every chain that holds me back from Thee;

> Thou art my all, and I love all in Thee;
> Thy voice like many waters calleth me.

Rawes

In the Blessed Sacrament the divine Face shines with supernal radiance. I adore Thee, most, holy Face, hidden beneath the eucharistic veil; O most august sacrament, by which Jesus our Saviour communicates to us all that He is and all that He has, I consecrate myself to Thee. Bind fast my heart, O sacramental God. With Magdalen, let me sit at Thy feet and bear Thee company in Thy loneliness. Burning with ardent love, I come to the table of the Lord. Let the voices of earth keep silence. Let mine eyes be closed to those things of time and sense which so long have held captive both mind and heart. I would see only Jesus, hear only Jesus. To Him whose love for me is eternal, I give my life, my heart, and my soul.

Ant. "I HAVE PURIFIED THEE AND PREPARED THEE. ARISE, GO SEEK FOR SOULS THAT I MAY REIGN OVER THEM. CHILD OF MY HEART, HAVE COURAGE AND CONFIDENCE. IMPRINT MY WORDS UPON THY SOUL."

V. I WILL GIVE THEE MY NAME TO BE THY LIGHT IN DARKNESS, AND THY STRENGTH IN THE DAY OF BATTLE.

R. Wash me, Lord Jesus, "not only my feet, but my hands and my head," that I may be worthy to labor in Thy service.

V. The Name of the Lord is wonderful, and above all names.

R. Come, let us bow before it.

Let us pray.

Eternal Father, I offer Thee the Holy Face of Our Lord. May it appease Thy just anger. Remember how it was crowned with thorns for our sins, and how it set itself as a rock to meet and break the waves of Thy justice, that we might be spared.

Look upon the wounds of Jesus. Unceasingly they plead for mercy—-for mercy on those who have rebelled against Thee.

V. O most sweet Face of Jesus, have compassion on our misery.

R. Mother most loving, plead for us with Jesus; convert us, and save us.

St. Michael, pray for us.

St. Veronica, pray for us.

May the souls of the faithful departed through the mercy of God rest in peace. Amen.

SUNDAY

SEXT

V. His mighty Name shall be our shield.

R. And His adorable Face shall be our fortress.

Glory be to the Father.

Hymn

Beneath the blows He stood, the mire and spittle on His Face,

With form so crushed, as if His heart were welling tears.

There came a look so full of tenderness

And on His precious mouth there spoke the pity of a soul divine.

Who could withstand that look?

Gethsemani[1]

O most sweet Redeemer, my love goes out to Thy Holy Face, disfigured in Thy Passion. In it I find the model for my imitation, the source of all love, the safeguard against sin, the motive for contrition. O loving Jesus, how can I offend Thee again when once Thy bleeding Face has taught me the malice of sin and the ingratitude of creatures?

The adorers of the Holy Face have been chosen to be the consolers of Jesus, outraged and reviled in His passion. Let us follow Him to Calvary.

Ant. "THE MALICE OF THE SIN OF BLASPHEMY IS BEYOND THY COMPREHENSION.

V. AH, IF THOU COULDST BUT CONCEIVE OF THE DEGREE OF GLORY THOU CANST MERIT BY SAYING ONLY ONCE, IN A SPIRIT OF REPARATION, "THE NAME OF THE LORD IS WONDERFUL!'

Eternal Father, I offer Thee the divine Heart of Jesus. Pour into it the wine of Thy justice, that it may be changed into the wine of mercy.

V. The Name of the Lord is wonderful, and above all names.

R. Come, let us bow down before it.

Let us pray.

Eternal Father, I offer Thee the Holy Face of Our Lord. May it appease Thy just anger. Remember how it was crowned with thorns for our sins, and how it set itself as a rock to meet and break the waves of Thy justice, that we might be spared.

Look upon the wounds of Jesus. Unceasingly they plead for mercy—-for mercy on those who have rebelled against Thee.

---

1. Right Rev. Msgr. Thomas S. Preston, V.G.

V. O most sweet Face of Jesus, have compassion on our misery.

R. Mother most loving, plead for us with Jesus; convert us, and save us.

St. Michael, pray for us.

St. Veronica, pray for us.

May the souls of the faithful departed through the mercy of God rest in peace. Amen.

Sunday

None

V. His mighty Name shall be our shield.

R. And His adorable Face shall be our fortress.

Glory be to the Father.

Hymn

Deep love, wide love, unchangeable and true,

Flows from the Sacred Heart, that burning shrine

Of faith, and hope, and peace, and love divine;

Gifts old arid new

The Bridegroom giveth ever to His bride,

As in her royal love she sitteth ever by His side.

Thou art the joy of souls, O Sacred Heart!

Their hope in darkness, light beyond the grave,

And strength in weariness, for Thou canst save;

To us Thou art

Far more than the great universe can be, a home of love, a city of the

free.

Rawes

God of compassion, look with pity on those who are far from Thee,
ensnared by passion and beguiled by the deceiving voices of the age.
Too often from inconstancy and frivolity we are negligent in Thy
service. And Thou, like a tender, patient father, dost correct us and
lead us back to Thee.

But there are sins which would tear God from His throne.
Rebellion against the teaching of the Church and blasphemy against
the holy Name attack the majesty of God. Those who deny Thee, resist
Thine omnipotence, outrage Thy goodness, and trample underfoot
the Precious Blood of Christ.

Their sins cry to heaven for vengeance and draw upon the earth the
thunderbolts of Thy justice.

O Father, so grievously offended, for all unbelieving, blaspheming
souls, I offer Thee the gracious, gentle words that fell from the lips of
Jesus. And with them I offer Thee all the words of prayer and praise
uttered by the adorers of Thy Holy Face.

Ant. "SIN HAS REACHED ITS CLIMAX. EVEN CHILDREN
BLASPHEME MY HOLY NAME."

O my God, I offer myself in reparation. All Thou hast given, I
would give; all for all.

V. The Name of the Lord is wonderful, arid worthy to be praised and exalted above all forever.

R. Come, let us adore it.

Let us pray.

Eternal Father, I offer Thee the Holy Face of Our Lord. May it appease Thy just anger. Remember how it was crowned with thorns for our sins, and how it set itself as a rock to meet and break the waves of Thy justice, that we might be spared.

Look upon the wounds of Jesus. Unceasingly they plead for mercy—-for mercy on those who have rebelled against Thee.

V. O most sweet Face of Jesus, have compassion on our misery.

R. Mother most loving, plead for us with Jesus; convert us, and save us.

St. Michael, pray for us.

St. Veronica, pray for us.

May the souls of the faithful departed through the mercy of God rest in peace. Amen.

Sunday

Vespers

V. His mighty Name shall be our shield.

R. And His adorable Face shall be our fortress.

Glory be to the Father.

Hymn

Ah, Lord, my light, my living breath,

Take me, oh, take me from this death,

And burst the bars that sever me

From my true life above;

Think how I die Thy Face to see,

And cannot live away from Thee,

O my eternal Love!

And ever, ever, weep and sigh,

Dying, because I do not die!

St. Teresa

How ingenious are the devices of the love of Jesus! He invites us to the work of reparation, and thereby opens a fountain of grace and sanctification to our souls. He shows us His Face and the fruits of His Passion, to make us understand the value of suffering, lovingly accepted and patiently endured.

Alas, that still Jesus should suffer! Alas, that there are still so many like unto Judas, all too eager to sell Thee for some trifling gain, some passing pleasure!

Lord, what wilt Thou have me to do? Let Thy Heart speak to mine. Fill it with sympathy, generosity, and love. I will love what Thou lovest and I will hate what Thou dost hate. With all my being I will labor for Thy honor and glory.

Ant. I WILL GIVE THEE MY ADORABLE FACE, AND WHEN THOU SHALT OFFER IT TO MY FATHER, MY LIPS SHALL PLEAD FOR THEE.

V. MY FACE SHALL BE THE VISIBLE SIGN OF REPARATION.

R. O Jesus, I love Thee above all earthly things, because Thou art infinitely worthy of being loved.

V. The name of the Lord is wonderful, and worthy to be praised and exalted above all forever.

R. Come, let us adore it.

Let us pray.

Eternal Father, I offer Thee the Holy Face of Our Lord. May it appease Thy just anger. Remember how it was crowned with thorns

for our sins, and how it set itself as a rock to meet and break the waves of Thy justice, that we might be spared.

Look upon the wounds of Jesus. Unceasingly they plead for mercy—-for mercy on those who have rebelled against Thee.

V. O most sweet Face of Jesus, have compassion on our misery.

R. Mother most loving, plead for us with Jesus; convert us, and save us.

St. Michael, pray for us.

St. Veronica, pray for us.

May the souls of the faithful departed through the mercy of God rest in peace. Amen.

Sunday

Compline

V. Lord, send forth the light of Thy Face upon Thy servants.

R. And save them according to Thy mercy.

V. His mighty Name shall be our shield.

R. And His adorable Face shall be our fortress.

Glory be to the Father.

Hymn

Ah, Lord, Thy woes belong,

Thy cruel pains, to me:

The burden of my sin and wrong
Hath all been laid on Thee.

Look on me where I kneel,
Wrath were my rightful lot,
One glance of love, O let me feel;
Redeemer, spurn me not!

O Jesus, eternal Truth and Wisdom, there was a day when we did not seek Thy Holy Face in reparation, nor even in contrition. And. the Father stretched forth the arm of His justice. He took back His gifts, and evil befell us. O adorable Face, behold the desolation of Thy people. Behold the chastisements that have fallen upon us because we have been ungrateful, because we have not known Thee in Thy gifts, because we have not loved Thee. O Jesus unknown, Jesus forgotten, Jesus all mercy and compassion, pardon us and receive us to the kiss of peace, for Thy holy Name's sake.

Ant. "MY CHILD, I GIVE THEE MY FACE AND MY HEART. I GIVE THEE MY BLOOD AND MY WOUNDS. TAKE OF THEM AND GIVE TO OTHERS."

V. I GIVE THEE MY FACE IN THE PRESENCE OF MY FATHER, IN THE STRENGTH OF THE HOLY SPIRIT, IN THE SIGHT OF THE ANGELS AND SAINTS OF GOD.
R. Strengthen my will, O Lord; for I am as nothing before Thee, incapable of aught but sin, without the assistance of Thy grace.
V. The Name of God is wonderful, and worthy to be praised and exalted above all forever.
R. Come, let us adore it.

Let us pray.

Eternal Father, I offer Thee the Holy Face of Our Lord. May it appease Thy just anger. Remember how it was crowned with thorns

for our sins, and how it set itself as a rock to meet and break the waves of Thy justice, that we might be spared.

Look upon the wounds of Jesus. Unceasingly they plead for mercy—-for mercy on those who have rebelled against Thee.

V. O most sweet Face of Jesus, have compassion on our misery.

R. Mother most loving, plead for us with Jesus; convert us, and save us.

St. Michael, pray for us.

St. Veronica, pray for us.

May the souls of the faithful departed through the mercy of God rest in peace. Amen.

Prayer

O Jesus, Thou art surely God to bear with us and dwell so patiently among us. How few there are who have the courage to range themselves under Thy standard and do battle with those who lead Thee again to Calvary!

As in the days of Thy passion. Thou art alone in the hands. of Thine enemies. Alas, if we have not the gift of tears like St. Peter, at least let us beat our breasts with the multitude returning to Jerusalem and acknowledging that "indeed this was the Son of God." O Holy Spirit, enliven us, and give us courage to throw ourselves in the vanguard of the strife. Give us the victory, and let all hearts own Thee for their king.

V. Adorable Jesus, teach us to compassionate Thy sufferings on earth, that we may merit to have a share in Thy glory in heaven.

R. This Face so marred and bruised shall one day appear, radiant in glory, and its enemies shall be annihilated forever.

V. The spirits of evil shall be driven back into darkness, and the Holy Face shall reign upon earth.

Blessed art thou, O Israel. Who is like unto thee, O people that art saved by the Lord, the shield of thy help, the sword of thy glory! Thine enemies shall deny thee and thou shalt tread upon their necks.

Lord, let us walk in the light of Thy Face, and rejoice day and night in the praise of Thy Name.

V. May the souls of the faithful departed through the mercy of God rest in peace.

R. And may the chains be broken that hold them captive far from Thy Face. Amen.

MONDAY

MATINS

Hail Mary.

O Jesus, Thou hast promised all good gifts to those who adore Thy Holy Face, in reparation for blasphemies uttered against Thy holy Name and the teachings of Thy Church.

Offer to the eternal Father, we implore Thee, these prayers which we pour forth to Thee for the greater glory of God and the conversion of sinners. Our Father, who art in heaven, look not upon us only, but upon the Face of Thy Christ.

V. O Lord, show us Thy Face and we shall be saved.

R. Turn Thy Face towards us and give us peace.

V. His mighty Name shall be our shield.

R. And His adorable Face shall be our fortress.

Glory be to the Father.

Hymn

Blood is the price of heaven,

All sins that price exceeds;

Oh, come to be forgiven:

He bleeds,

My Saviour bleeds,

Bleeds!

Under the olive boughs,

Falling like ruby beads,

The blood drops from His brow:

He bleeds,

My Saviour bleeds,

Bleeds!

Faber

Dear Jesus, Thy Holy Face is lying in the dust. Ungrateful earth is drinking the Precious Blood that oozes from Thy sacred brow. Thy soul is overwhelmed with mortal anguish. Thy friends are asleep, Thy gifts and graces all forgotten. Only hatred wakes, and Satan sharpens the sword of Thine enemies.

"Could ye not watch with Me one, hour, ye that called one on the other to die for Me? Or see ye not Judas, how that he sleepeth not, but maketh haste to betray Me to the Jews? Why sleep ye? Rise and pray, lest ye enter into temptation."

O my forsaken Jesus, let me be Thy comforter in this hour of sorrow. I offer Thee for Thy refreshment the wine of love and reparation. Let it assuage Thy thirst for souls. Take my poor, timid heart. Make it divine. Strengthen its weakness. Awaken it from its sleep of cowardice and ingratitude, and let it pour upon Thy sacred grounds a balm more precious than all the perfumes of earth.

Ant. LIKE AN ARROW I HOLD THEE IN MY HANDS. I WILL BEND THE BOW AND SPEED THEE AMONG MY ENEMIES."

V. "God wills not the death of a sinner, but rather that he turn from his wickedness and live."

R. Father, forgive them, for they know not what they do.

Let us Pray

THE GOLDEN ARROW[1]

May the most holy, most sacred, most adorable Name of God be ever praised, blessed, loved, adored, and glorified, in heaven, on earth, and under the earth, by all creatures, and by the Sacred Heart of our Lord Jesus Christ in the most holy sacrament of the altar. Amen.

V. Lord, hide us within the secret of Thy Face, and have mercy upon us for the glory of Thy holy Name.

R. I accept all the sufferings Thou shalt send upon me for the glory of Thy Name and the conversion of sinners.

V. Blessed be the Holy Face in the sweat of blood.

R. May the Precious Blood purify the souls of the faithful departed and bring them to the shining of the perpetual light. Amen.

---

1. Revealed to Sr. Marie de St. Pierre.

Monday

Lauds

℣. His mighty Name shall be our shield.

R. And His adorable Face shall be our fortress.

Glory be to the Father.

Hymn

I heard the tramp of arms,

The shouts that rose on every side,

Like voices from the depths of hell;

I saw the sad procession move:

They led the way to Calvary;

Their spears were pointing to the hill.

My blessed Lord was passing from my sight;

I fell upon my knees and kissed the ground His feet had trod.

Gethsemani

Men have stood up in battle array to fight against the Lord, their God and their King. Their tongues have distilled venom. They have said, We know no master; we will not have this man to reign over us; we will drag His glory to the earth, and the power of His Name we will destroy.

But Lord, Thy Name is above all names and beyond all human power. Thou dost laugh at the schemes of the wicked. With a breath Thou canst bring thein to naught, with a look Thou canst grind Thine enemies to powder.

But in Thy divine compassion Thou dost wait for them and bear with them that Thou mayest have mercy on them.

And we, Thy servants, will go forth to meet them, bearing the standard of the Holy Face and armed; with the love of the Sacred Heart.

Ant. "I HAVE BEEN TORN FROM THE TABERNACLE, AND MY SANCTUARIES HAVE BEEN PROFANED. THE HANDS OF MINE ENEMIES HAVE BEEN LAID UPON THE LORD'S ANOINTED."

V. "Have they not committed the crime of Judas? They have sold Me for money."

R. Eternal Father, I take for arms against Thine enemies the cross of Jesus Christ and the instruments of His holy Passion, and I pray Thee to put division among them, for Thy blessed Son hath said, "A house divided against itself cannot stand."

V. "God wills not the death of a sinner, but rather that he turn from his wickedness and live."

R. Father, forgive them, for they know not what they do.

Let us pray.

THE GOLDEN ARROW

May the most holy, most sacred, most adorable Name of God be ever praised, blessed, loved, adored, and glorified, in heaven, on earth, and under the earth, by all creatures, and by the Sacred Heart of our Lord Jesus Christ in the most holy sacrament of the altar. Amen.

V. Lord, hide us within the secret of Thy Face, and have mercy upon us for the glory of Thy holy Name.

R. I accept all the sufferings Thou shalt send upon me for the glory of Thy Name and the conversion of sinners.

V. Blessed be the Holy Face in the sweat of blood.

R. May the Precious Blood purify the souls of the faithful departed and bring them to the shining of the perpetual light. Amen.

Monday

Prime

V. His mighty Name shall be our shield.

R. And His adorable Face shall be our fortress.

Glory be to the Father.

Hymn

O thou Mother dear! pray to Jesus
For all helpfulness of grace;
O thou blest one! bring thy children
To the vision of His Face.

Then, when this long night, of sorrow,

With its pain, hath passed away,

We shall see thee crowned, in glory.

Midst the splendors of the day.

Rawes

Arise, Lord, and let Thine enemies be scattered, and let all that hate Thee flee before Thy Face,

May the thrice holy Name of God overthrow their counsels. May the awful Name of the eternal God annihilate their impiety.

O my God, arise, defend the cause that is Thine as well as mine. Abandon us not to the rage of Thine enemies. Let them not triumph over us. Give unto us, one day, the joy of seeing those that hate Thee now praise and adore and love Thy holy Name.

Ant. "THEY ARE THE ENEMIES OF MY CROSS. TAKE IT WITH THE INSTRUMENS OF MY PASSION FOR YOUR PANOPLY OF WAR.

V. "The arms of My enemies deal death, but Mine give life."

R. The Blessed Virgin Mary shall hold the weapons wherewith her Soil hath armed me for the fight. She is the Tower of David where hang a thousand bucklers.

V. God wills not the death of a sinner, but rather that he turn from his wickedness and live.

R. Father, forgive them, for they know not what they do.

Let us pray.

THE GOLDEN ARROW

May the most holy, most sacred, most adorable Name of God be ever praised, blessed, loved, adored, and glorified, in heaven, on earth, and under the earth, by all creatures, and by the Sacred Heart of our Lord Jesus Christ in the most holy sacrament of the altar. Amen.

V. Lord, hide us within the secret of Thy Face, and have mercy upon us for the glory of Thy holy Name.

R. I accept all the sufferings Thou shalt send upon me for the glory of Thy Name and the conversion of sinners.

V. Blessed be the Holy Face in the sweat of blood.

R. May the Precious Blood purify the souls of the faithful departed and bring them to the shining of the perpetual light. Amen.

MONDAY

TIERCE

V. His mighty Name; shall be our shield.
R. And His adorable Face shall be our fortress.
Glory be. to the Father.

Hymn

Sing, my tongue, the glorious battle,
With completed victory rise;
And above the cross's trophy
Tell the triumph of the strife:

How the world's Redeemer conquered
By surrendering of life.

In ages past, courageous armies went forth to fight the battles of the Lord in the Holy Land. His faithful servant, St. Bernard, preached this glorious crusade. Kings and people rose up at the sound of his voice and marched with one accord to the rescue of the holy places, sanctified by the life and death of our Redeemer.

Our Lord calls us now to a new crusade, and shall we be deaf to His voice? He asks us not to leave our native land. No need to arm with sword arid buckler. In this holy war the cross of Jesus Christ shall be our weapon, both of offense and defense. In this sign we conquer. Our trust is in the Name of the Lord who hath made heaven and earth, and "God forbid that we should glory save in the cross of our Lord Jesus Christ."

Our glorious Mother will bless our arms. She herself will lead the soldiers of Christ, for is she not "more terrible than an army set in battle array"?

Ant. "I WILL NOT STAY WITH THIS UNGRATEFUL PEOPLE. BEHOLD THE TORRENT OF MY TEARS!"

V. "ARE THERE NONE TO WIPE THEM AWAY? NONE TO OFFER REPARATION TO THE OFFENDED JUSTICE OF GOD? NONE TO BEG FOR THE CONVERSION OF SINNERS?"

R. With the ever-blessed Virgin-Mother of God, with St. Joseph and all the holy angels, let us adore the Holy Face in reparation for the outrages offered to God by the enemies of the cross.

V. God wills not the death of a sinner, but rather that he turn from his wickedness and live.

R. Father, forgive them, for they know not what they do.

Let us pray.

THE GOLDEN ARROW

May the most holy, most sacred, most adorable Name of God be ever praised, blessed, loved, adored, and glorified, in heaven, on earth, and under the earth, by all creatures, and by the Sacred Heart of our Lord Jesus Christ in the most holy sacrament of the altar. Amen.

V. Lord, hide us within the secret of Thy Face, and have mercy upon us for the glory of Thy holy Name.

R. I accept all the sufferings Thou shalt send upon me for the glory of Thy Name and the conversion of sinners.

V. Blessed be the Holy Face in the sweat of blood.

R. May the Precious Blood purify the souls of the faithful departed and bring them to the shining of the perpetual light. Amen.

MONDAY

SEXT

V. His mighty Name shall be our shield.

R. And His adorable Face shall be our fortress.

Glory be to the Father.

Hymn

The ruffians came once more
To beat Him with their hands,
To spit upon His swollen Face,
To press the agonizing crown
Upon His temples, gashed and raw,

To mock His tears, to strike Him with
His reed of straw.

Gethsemani

I contemplate the Holy Face of Jesus, and I mark the suffering love imprinted there. As I study its blessed features, my love grows, and strength and grace to do God's work increase with love. In this great work of reparation, expiation, and intercession, our Lord opens to us a mine of gold and He invites us all to labor there with fervent zeal. "Why stand ye here all the day idle?" Is there a work more glorious? Behold the priceless treasures hidden there! Souls, souls, are the price of your labor! Souls which cost the shedding of the blood of Christ! What reward have you, you who live for the world? What do you gain, you who early and late seek for riches? What shall it profit you, you who live for self and the gratification, of its appetites? Behold, I give you souls! Souls that shall live eternally. And "I will give you what is just." I will give you heavenly treasure, wherewith you shall purchase your own soul and the souls that are dear to you.

O how good Thou art, my Jesus! Thy heart is ever yearning for souls, even for those that revile Thee and trample upon Thy Precious Blood.

Praise and glory be to God for His incomprehensible mercy!

Ant. OH, IF THEY KNEW THE TREASURES BURIED IN THIS MINE, THE LABORERS WOULD NOT BE SO FEW.

V. UNLOVING IS THE HEART THAT DOES NOT KINDLE AT THE THOUGHT OF A WORK SO GLORIOUS, SO ACCEPTABLE TO ME.

R. Lord, glorify Thyself in our weakness. Let all the heavenly court praise Thee, that by such humble instruments Thou dost accomplish a work so mighty.

"And He said: My grace is sufficient for thee; for power is made perfect in infirmity. Gladly therefore will I glory in my infirmities, that the power of Christ may dwell in me. When I am weak, then am I powerful."[1]

V. God wills not the death of a sinner, but rather that he turn from his wickedness and live.

R. Father, forgive them, for they know not what they do.

Let us pray.

THE GOLDEN ARROW

May the most holy, most sacred, most adorable Name of God be ever praised, blessed, loved, adored, and glorified, in heaven, on earth, and under the earth, by all creatures, and by the Sacred Heart of our Lord Jesus Christ in the most holy sacrament of the altar. Amen.

V. Lord, hide us within the secret of Thy Face, and have mercy upon us for the glory of Thy holy Name.

R. I accept all the sufferings Thou shalt send upon me for the glory of Thy Name and the conversion of sinners.

V. Blessed be the Holy Face in the sweat of blood.

R. May the Precious Blood purify the souls of the faithful departed and bring them to the shining of the perpetual light. Amen.

---

1. 2 Cor. xii. 9, 10.

Monday

None

V. His mighty Name shall be our shield.

R. And His adorable Face shall be our fortress.

Glory be to the Father.

Hymn

There came a ray of light, and in its beams

I saw again His blessed Face.

He stood in bonds before the judgment throne.

His eyes were looking up as if to scenes beyond the earth.

There was a sadness dark as night upon His brow,

> While peace that seemed the eternal calm of God
> Was reigning there.

Gethsemani

O sacred Face, from the Praetorium as from a throne, Thou dost establish Thy deathless reign.

But alas for those who refuse to bear Thine easy yoke and burden light! Alas for those who rebel against Thee, O Jesus, King of peace! The world has gone after its idols and God is despised. Who is there to defend the interests of Him who is their benefactor, their friend, and their saviour?

O ye who trample underfoot the Precious Blood of Christ, O ye who sit down to eat and rise up to play, O ye who glory in your strength, your riches, and your wisdom, the calm, patient Face of Jesus looks upon you and waits. God is not mocked. Whatsoever ye sow that shall ye also reap. The end is not yet. God will arise. He will not always plead. That suffering, loving Face will become stern and terrible when your day of grace shall have passed. "O Jesus! be not my judge, but my Saviour."

Ant. "THE FACE OF THE EARTH HAS BECOME HIDEOUS IN THE DIVINE EYES. THE JUSTICE OF THE FATHER IS AROUSED. OFFER HIM THE FACE OF HIS SON, THAT COMPASSION MAY TAKE THE PLACE OF WRATH."

V. In the face of the Saviour is your salvation.

R. Turn to the Blessed Mother of God. She is the dispenser of grace. Tell her we are her children by every right and title.

V. God wills not the death of the sinner, but rather that he turn from his wickedness and live.

R. Father, forgive them, for they know not what they do.

Let us pray.

THE GOLDEN ARROW

May the most holy, most sacred, most adorable Name of God be ever praised, blessed, loved, adored, and glorified, in heaven, on earth, and under the earth, by all creatures, and by the Sacred Heart of our Lord Jesus Christ in the most holy sacrament of the altar. Amen.

V. Lord, hide us within the secret of Thy Face, and have mercy upon us for the glory of Thy holy Name.

R. I accept all the sufferings Thou shalt send upon me for the glory of Thy Name and the conversion of sinners.

V. Blessed be the Holy Face in the sweat of blood.

R. May the Precious Blood purify the souls of the faithful departed and bring them to the shining of the perpetual light. Amen.

MONDAY

VESPERS

V. His mighty Name shall be our shield.

R. And His adorable Face shall be our fortress.

Glory be to the Father.

Hymn

Thus despised, thus desecrated,

Thus in dying desolated,

Slain for me of sinners vilest,

Loving Lord, on me Thou smilest;

Shine forth, bright Face, and strengthen me!

O Jesus, my beloved, let my praises bring joy to Thy sorrowful Face. Show me Thy Face beaming with gladness and resplendent with glory! We praise and adore Thy glorious name of Redeemer.

That is Thy dearest title, the title of predilection, the one above all others that claims our love.

Thou hast redeemed us and made us a people, to our God, but Thou hast done more. Thou hast given us Thyself to be our food by the way. Thou hast, not left us comfortless. Thou art "with us all days," in days of toil and days of rest, in days of sorrow and days of joy, in days of care and anxiety and days of hope.

O Jesus, in the adorable sacrament of the altar, Thine august Face is shining with light ineffable. We adore Thee, we praise Thee, we love Thee for Thy great glory, O sacramental God, O Jesus, beloved above all others.

May our prayers and penances obtain grace for our own. souls and pardon for those who love Thee not. We long to see Thee loved. Let this desire return unto our own hearts and make them like unto Thine. O Thou divine Lover of souls, again and again we implore Thee for those who grieve Thee most. We fear not to "offend Thee by our continual coming." These souls have cost Thee so dear, sweet Lord, we cannot let Thee go except Thou bless them. Have compassion on the multitude and save them.

Ant. A Man of sorrows and acquainted with grief, Christ was crowned with thorns. The same is He that crowneth us with mercy and compassion.

V. He was wounded for our transgressions. He was bruised for our sins..

R. Reparation is the most perfect imitation of Jesus Christ. Jesus, my Saviour, I live for the greater glory of God and the salvation of souls.

V. God wills not the death of a sinner, but rather that he turn from his wickedness and live.

R. Father, forgive them, for they know not what they do.

Let us pray.

THE GOLDEN ARROW

May the most holy, most sacred, most adorable Name of God be ever praised, blessed, loved, adored, and glorified, in heaven, on earth, and under the earth, by all creatures, and by the Sacred Heart of our Lord Jesus Christ in the most holy sacrament of the altar. Amen.

V. Lord, hide us within the secret of Thy Face, and have mercy upon us for the glory of Thy holy Name.

R. I accept all the sufferings Thou shalt send upon me for the glory of Thy Name and the conversion of sinners.

V. Blessed be the Holy Face in the sweat of blood.

R. May the Precious Blood purify the souls of the faithful departed and bring them to the shining of the perpetual light. Amen.

MONDAY

COMPLINE

V. His mighty Name shall be our shield.

R. And His adorable Face shall be our fortress.

Glory be to the Father.

Hymn

Two hands have haunted me for days,

Two hands of slender shape,

All crushed and torn, as in the press

Is bruised the purple grape;

At work or meals, at prayer or play,

Those mangled palms I see,
And a plaintive voice keeps whispering,
"These hands were pierced for thee!"
For me, sweet Lord, for me?"
Yea, even so, ungrateful thing!
These hands were pierced for thee!

E. C. Donnelly

Sin! Sin! God always offended, God' always grieved! The Precious Blood always despised and trampled underfoot! Lord, shall it never cease? Wilt Thou never see of the travail of Thy soul and be satisfied? O God of compassion, how can a heart that loves Thee find rest except in reparation and expiation! How can I rejoice when my Master weeps!

Lord, I am Thine. I offer myself a holocaust and a victim. Take me and fashion me to Thy liking. Use me when and where Thou needest me. Only let me bring a smile to the Face of my Saviour. Only let me bring one heart to His sacred feet. My poor and worthless life shall have offered Thee a little joy, a little reparation. A humble wayside flower, Thou wilt not despise its perfume.

Ant. Christ suffered for us, leaving us an example, that we should follow in His steps.

R. Thou hast turned for Me my mourning into rejoicing.
V. "The blessing of the Father, and the Son, and the Holy Ghost be upon thy mission.
R. "THOU SHALT INDEED DRINK OF MY CHALICE, BUT I WILL HOLD IT FOR THEE."

Let us Pray

Lord, Thou speakest to my soul. How shall I be worthy of Thee? I give myself to Thee; do with me whatsoever Thou wilt. O sweet Saviour, would that I might even drink of the bitter cup reserved for sinners, if thus they might be spared! But alas! what am I that I should stay the wrath of God? I who am nothingness and misery. Yet out of nothing Thou didst create the world. Deign, then, to make use of me, *even me,* to do the work of God. Amen.

V. God will unite mercy and justice.

R. Lord, let me rejoice in Thy salvation.

V. "God forbid that I should glory save in the cross of my, Lord Jesus Christ."

R. O my God, let sinners be hidden in the secret of Thy Face. Have mercy on them for the glory of Thy Name.

V. May the souls of the faithful departed by the mercy of God rest in peace.

R. And may they sing in heaven the praises of the Holy Face.

Let us pray.

THE GOLDEN ARROW

May the most holy, most sacred, most adorable Name of God be ever praised, blessed, loved, adored, and glorified, in heaven, on earth, and under the earth, by all creatures, and by the Sacred Heart of our Lord Jesus Christ in the most holy sacrament of the altar. Amen.

V. Lord, hide us within the secret of Thy Face, and have mercy upon us for the glory of Thy holy Name.

R. I accept all the sufferings Thou shalt send upon me for the glory of Thy Name and the conversion of sinners.

V. Blessed be the Holy Face in the sweat of blood.

R. May the Precious Blood purify the souls of the faithful departed and bring them to the shining of the perpetual light. Amen.

Prayer. O Jesus, Thou art God, p. 16.

TUESDAY

MATINS

Hail Mary.

O Jesus, Thou hast promised all good gifts to those who adore
Thy Holy Face in reparation for blasphemies uttered against Thy holy
Name and the teaching of Thy Church.

Offer to the eternal Father, we implore Thee, these prayers which
we pour forth to Thee for the greater glory of God and the conversion
of sinners. Our Father who art in heaven, look not upon us only, but
upon the Face of Thy Christ.

V. O Lord, show us Thy Face, and we shall be saved.

R. Turn Thy Face towards us, and give us peace.

V. His mighty Name shall be our shield.

R. And His adorable Face shall be our fortress.

Glory be to the Father.

Hymn

Why must I win you by My tears?

Why must I touch you with a bleeding hand?

Why must I break the idols of the earth,

And make your home so desolate?

Why can I not win you by the beauty of My Face?

Why must the bitterness of sin bring souls to Me?

Why must I bear them on My bleeding shoulders

as My cross?

Gethsemani

Divine Master, Thou dost open to us the way of sorrow, and our sensuous nature shrinks from it. Our fastidiousness, our self-seeking, our desires for earthly goods, all lead us in another path. When Thou leadest us to Thabor, to joy, and to gladness, we follow Thee willingly, but to Calvary with its ignominies, its suffering and death? Oh, no, not there, Lord, not there. This is the cry of nature. Of the natural man it is always true that "Jesus hath many lovers of His heavenly kingdom, but few that are willing to bear His cross." He has many that are desirous of comfort, but few of tribulation.

Yet to the lover of the sorrowful Face of Jesus, the compassionate tenderness and suffering love imprinted there, are more winning than the radiance of the transfigured Face of Thabor.

Ant. "My child, behold the wounds inflicted upon Me by sinners."

V. "IF MY JUSTICE, WERE NOT RESTRAINED BY MERCY, THE GUILTY WOULD BE ANNIHILATED, AND EVEN

INANIMATE CREATURES WOULD FALL UPON THEM AND DESTROY THEM."

V. O Holy Face of Jesus, give me a great love for the mystery of the cross.

R. And enkindle in my heart the spirit of reparation.

Let us Pray

O adorable Face of my Jesus, so mercifully bowed down on the tree of the cross, on the day of Thy Passion, for the salvation of men, now again incline in Thy pity towards us poor sinners; cast upon us a look of compassion, and receive us to the kiss of peace.

V. O heart of mine, have thou but one desire, to console thy Jesus.

R. Let us rejoice that we may watch before His Holy Face.

V. Lord, I am weak, but Thou art strong.

R. If I watch before Him, I shall love Him. If I love Him I shall obey Him.

V. May the souls of the faithful departed rest in peace.

R. Through the mercy of God.

Amen.

TUESDAY

LAUDS

V. His mighty Name shall be our shield.

R. And His adorable Face shall be our fortress.

Glory be to the Father.

Hymn

Hail to Thee, Thou head of mourning!
Crowned with thorns for pain and scorning:
Mocked and bleeding; broken, wounded,
Spat upon, by foes surrounded;
Bruised with the rod's indignity.

Hail to Thee, from whose resplendent

Face has fled the light transcendent;

Lo, Thy splendor paling, pining;

Thou, before whose awful shining

Heaven's cohorts quake and bow the knee!

O Jesus, Son of the living God, I adore Thee and praise Thee for all the outrages endured in the Passion, in all the members of Thy sacred body. But more especially I adore the sufferings of Thy sacred Face.

I greet Thee; sweet Face of Jesus, bruised with blows and soiled with spittle and dust.

I greet you, O beautiful eyes, bathed with tears and beaming with love arid compassion,

I greet you, blessed lips, uttering words of pardon and promise.

I greet you, ye precious tears, falling upon the sterile earth and bidding it bring forth fruit for life eternal.

Ant. My blood is the price of souls.

V. What grief to the Sacred Heart to see that blood despised!

R. "BLASPHEMIES HAVE PIERCED THE HEART OF THE SAVIOUR TILL IT HAS BECOME A MASS OF BLEEDING WOUNDS."

V. O Holy Face, give me a great love for the mystery of the cross.

R. And enkindle in my heart the spirit of reparation.

Let us pray.

O adorable Face of my Jesus, so mercifully bowed down on the tree of the cross, on the day of Thy Passion, for the salvation of men, now again incline in Thy pity towards us poor sinners; cast upon us a look of compassion, and receive us to the kiss of peace.

V. O heart of mine, have thou but one desire, to console thy Jesus.

R. Let us rejoice that we may watch before His Holy Face.

V. Lord, I am weak, but Thou art strong.

R. If I watch before Him, I shall love Him. If I love Him I shall obey Him.

V. May the souls of the faithful departed rest in peace.

R. Through the mercy of God.

Amen.

TUESDAY

PRIME

V. His mighty Name shall be our shield.

R. And His adorable Face shall be our fortress.

Glory be to the Father.

Hymn

When by Thee my soul is bidden,
Let not then Thy Face be hidden!
Lover whom 'tis life to cherish,
Shine and leave me not to perish!
Bend from Thy cross and succor me.

"And they blindfolded Him and smote Him on the Face."

Those penetrating eyes struck terror to the hearts of our Lord's persecutors. While They were fixed upon them their satanic rage was stayed against their will. So the sinner who would give the reins to his passions denies the existence of God. He shrinks before the searching eyes of the Omniscient, and he quiets his heart, saying: "God doth not see, there is no God." But he blindfolds himself only, while God looks on and says: "Behold Mine eyes have seen all these things, and Mine ears have heard them, and I have understood them all."

Ant. ASK OF MY FATHER AS MANY SOULS AS I HAVE SHED DROPS OF MY PRECIOUS BLOOD.

Ant. WHENEVER THOU DOST OFFER MY HOLY FACE TO THE FATHER, MY LIPS BEG FOR MERCY.

V. O Holy Face, give me a great love for the mystery of the cross.

R. And enkindle in My heart the spirit of reparation.

Let us pray.

O adorable Face of my Jesus, so mercifully bowed down on the tree of the cross, on the day of Thy Passion, for the salvation of men, now again incline in Thy pity towards us poor sinners; cast upon us a look of compassion, and receive us to the kiss of peace.

V. O heart of mine, have thou but one desire, to console thy Jesus.

R. Let us rejoice that we may watch before His Holy Face.

V. Lord, I am weak, but Thou art strong.

R. If I watch before Him, I shall love Him. If I love Him I shall obey Him.

V. May the souls of the faithful departed rest in peace.

R. Through the mercy of God.

Amen.

TUESDAY

TIERCE

V. His mighty Name shall be our shield.

R. And His adorable Face shall be our fortress.

Glory be to the Father.

Hymn

Jesu, who once for us hast died,

With wounded hands and feet and side,

We think of Thy great agony,

A pathless sea,

When Thou wast hanging crucified,

O burning love.

Rawes

O Jesus, sweet Redeemer, throughout that fearful night, ignominy and suffering were heaped upon Thy blessed head. Spittle and blows fell upon Thy sacred Face, and Thou wast silent. They tightened the cords that bound Thy hands till the blood spurted from every vein. They tore the hair from Thy sacred head and beard, and even under this indignity Thou wast silent. They sought to force a cry from Thy poor, discolored, bruised, and bleeding lips, but Thou didst utter no sound.

O Jesus, God thrice holy, thus didst Thou expiate words of impurity, imprecation, and unbelief.

Let us unite our silence to His, and may our words be so many acts of reparation. "The tongue is a fire, a world of iniquity. It is set on fire of hell." Jesus, make me patient, meek, humble, and compassionate, for out of the abundance of the heart the mouth speaketh.

Ant. "IN PROPORTION TO YOUR SPIRIT OF REPARATION I WILL RESTORE IN YOU MY IMAGE DISFIGURED BY SIN.

Ant. "I HAVE TAKEN UPON MY HEAD THE SINS OF MANKIND, THAT THE MEMBERS OF CHRIST MAY BE SPARED.

V. His sword shall be the beauty of His Holy Face. He shall conquer by humility. His shall be the glorious reign of love.

V. O Holy Face, give me a great love for the mystery of the cross.

R. And enkindle in my heart the spirit of reparation.

Let us pray.

O adorable Face of my Jesus, so mercifully bowed down on the tree of the cross, on the day of Thy Passion, for the salvation of men, now again incline in Thy pity towards us poor sinners; cast upon us a look of compassion, and receive us to the kiss of peace.

V. O heart of mine, have thou but one desire, to console thy Jesus.

R. Let us rejoice that we may watch before His Holy Face.

V. Lord, I am weak, but Thou art strong.

R. If I watch before Him, I shall love Him. If I love Him I shall obey Him.

V. May the souls of the faithful departed rest in peace.

R. Through the mercy of God.

Amen.

TUESDAY

SEXT

V. His mighty Name shall be our shield.

R. And His adorable Face shall be our fortress.

Glory be to the Father.

Hymn

Behold Me then a thorn-crowned King.

I rule by pain. I suffer for the pride of those I love.

It is a struggle long, a battle dire,

To conquer each rebellious foe,

That those who choose Me for their

Spouse May thus be truly one with Me.

That all self-love shall cease;

That they may have no thought but Mine.

Gethsemani

O King of heaven and earth, a filthy mantles covers Thy sacred form. The soldiers laugh and jeer at this coarse sarcasm. Thine august Face is calm and grave, hut among the Roman cohort there is not one who is touched with Thy patience, O suffering Lamb of God! Jesus is mocked, and shall I assert myself? Shall I be vain and proud? Shall I shrink from ridicule, contempt, or neglect?

Ant. THERE IS A ROD IN MY HAND, AND IT IS THE ROD OF MY JUSTICE.

V. IF YOU WOULD MAKE IT FALL HARMLESS, OFFER ME WORKS OF REPARATION.

R. In union with the whole Church I adore Thee, I love Thee, O Jesus of Nazareth, King of the Jews, full of grace and truth.

V. O Holy Face of Jesus, make me to understand the mystery of suffering and expiation.

R. And may I be consumed with the desire of suffering with Thee.

Let us pray.

O adorable Face of my Jesus, so mercifully bowed down on the tree of the cross, on the day of Thy Passion, for the salvation of men, now again incline in Thy pity towards us poor sinners; cast upon us a look of compassion, and receive us to the kiss of peace.

V. O heart of mine, have thou but one desire, to console thy Jesus.

R. Let us rejoice that we may watch before His Holy Face.

V. Lord, I am weak, but Thou art strong.

R. If I watch before Him, I shall love Him. If I love Him I shall obey Him.

V. May the souls of the faithful departed rest in peace.

R. Through the mercy of God.

Amen.

TUESDAY

NONE

Hymn

Hail, holy wounds of Jesus, hail!
Sweet pledges of the saving rood,
Whence flow the streams that never fail,
The purple streams of His dear blood.

His comely brow, O shame and grief,

By the sharp thorny crown is riven,

Through hands and feet, without relief,

The cruel nails are deeply driven.

And they platted a crown of thorns, and the soldiers pressed it down upon Thy head, and the sharp points were buried in the quivering flesh of the God-Man. They laughed at Him, and in scorn and satire they called Him a king.

O Jesus, king of glory, in that fearful night Thou wast a victim struggling with the justice of the Father, and, notwithstanding the crimes of men, Thy blood was victorious.

By those thorns which opened each a fountain of life, have mercy on those whose unbelief and pride of opinion crown Thee anew.

Ant. OFFER ME TO THE ETERNAL FATHER TO APPEASE HIS JUSTICE.

V. If you but knew the efficacy of the offering.

R. Each wound cries to heaven for mercy. O God, hearken and forgive.

V. O adorable Face, make me understand the mystery of suffering and expiation.

R. And may I be consumed with the desire of suffering with Thee.

Let us pray.

O adorable Face of my Jesus, so mercifully bowed down on the tree of the cross, on the day of Thy Passion, for the salvation of men, now again incline in Thy pity towards us poor sinners; cast upon us a look of compassion, and receive us to the kiss of peace.

V. O heart of mine, have thou but one desire, to console thy Jesus.

R. Let us rejoice that we may watch before His Holy Face.

V. Lord, I am weak, but Thou art strong.

R. If I watch before Him, I shall love Him. If I love Him I shall obey

Him.

    V. May the souls of the faithful departed rest in peace.

R. Through the mercy of God.

Amen.

TUESDAY

VESPERS

V. His mighty Name shall be our shield.

R. And His adorable Face shall be our fortress.

Glory be to the Father.

Hymn

Beneath the wine-press of God's wrath,

To save our souls from endless pains,

Still hour by hour His blood flows forth,

Till not a single drop remains.

> Come bathe you in that healing flood,
> All ye who mourn with sin opprest;
> Your only hope is Jesus' blood,
> His Sacred Heart's your only rest.

The executioners have placed a reed between the bound hands of Jesus, a sign of His helplessness. They strike Him and tear the hair from His sacred head. Patience of God, didst Thou bear this? Why need it have been? Mightest Thou not have been spared this? O long-suffering and most meek Saviour, we bow before Thine august Face, and in expiation of these outrages, and for those who mock and deride Thee and all that is sacred, we salute Thee and adore Thee with St. Gertrude: "Hail, living Pearl of the Divinity; I adore Thee, Thou incorruptible flower of our humanity."

Ant. "I AM THE LIBERATOR OF SOULS."

V. I RENEW IN THEM THE IMAGE OF GOD.

R. I am but a weak reed, but in the hands of Jesus Christ I shall be strong against the adversary.

V. Holy Face, make me understand the mystery of suffering and expiation.

R. And may I be consumed with the desire of suffering with Thee.

Let us pray.

O adorable Face of my Jesus, so mercifully bowed down on the tree of the cross, on the day of Thy Passion, for the salvation of men, now again incline in Thy pity towards us poor sinners; cast upon us a look of compassion, and receive us to the kiss of peace.

V. O heart of mine, have thou but one desire, to console thy Jesus.

R. Let us rejoice that we may watch before His Holy Face.

V. Lord, I am weak, but Thou art strong.

R. If I watch before Him, I shall love Him. If I love Him I shall obey Him.

V. May the souls of the faithful departed rest in peace.

R. Through the mercy of God.

Amen.

TUESDAY

COMPLINE

V. His mighty Name shall be our shield.

R. And His adorable Face shall be our fortress.

Glory be to the Father.

Hymn

I am traveling now the weary, sorrowing road,

The way that leads to Calvary.

So treading in my Bridegroom's steps, I journey on.

Falling, rising, fainting, weeping,

I am moving on. It is not I,

The self I knew is gone. I only know one life,

And in that life I see and feel and hear.

The Spirit guides my eyes, unfolds the graces of my Master dear,

And shows to me the beauties of His dying. Face,

The depths of pity infinite.

Gethsemani

O my Saviour, I contemplate Thy sufferings, and they teach me the infinite love which delivered Thee into the hands of Thine executioners.

O adorable Victim of the malice of men, accept our acts of mortification and humility, our ardent desires, and our silent sufferings, as so many reparations for the sins which abound on every side. The night has come when sin walks abroad. Listen, Lord, listen to the voice of prayer that ascends to Thee, for pardon and mercy. This night Thou wilt be mocked, Thou wilt be spit upon, and the scenes of Thy Passion will be renewed. Innocence will be lost, and crime will be added to crime before the morning dawns. Pardon, Lord, pardon and spare. Let not the sinner die in his sins.

Ant. I AM NOT KNOWN, I AM NOT LOVED. MY COMMANDMENTS ARE DESPISED.

V. THE STORM OF MY WRATH IS RISING, BUT IF A SOUL BE FAITHFUL I WILL NOT FORSAKE IT.

R. The Lord has bent His bow and He will speed His arrows. O Jesus, by Thy divine promises, have mercy on the souls dear to me.

V. Holy Face, make me understand the mystery of suffering and expiation.

R. And consume me with the desire of suffering with Thee.

Let us pray.

O adorable Face of my Jesus, so mercifully bowed down on the tree of the cross, on the day of Thy Passion, for the salvation of men, now again incline in Thy pity towards us poor sinners; cast upon us a look of compassion, and receive us to the kiss of peace.

V. O heart of mine, have thou but one desire, to console thy Jesus.

R. Let us rejoice that we may watch before His Holy Face.

V. Lord, I am weak, but Thou art strong.

R. If I watch before Him, I shall love Him. If I love Him I shall obey Him.

V. May the souls of the faithful departed rest in peace.

R. Through the mercy of God.

Amen.

WEDNESDAY

MATINS

Hail Mary.

O Jesus, Thou hast promised all good gifts to those who adore Thy Holy Face in reparation for blasphemies uttered against Thy holy Name and the teachings of Thy Church.

Offer to the eternal Father, we implore Thee, these prayers which we pour forth for the greater glory of God and the conversion of sinners.

Our Father who art in heaven, look not upon us only, but upon the Face of Thy Christ.

V. O Lord, show us Thy Face, and we shall be saved.

R. Turn Thy Face towards us and give us peace.

V. His mighty Name shall be our shield.

R. And His adorable Face shall be our fortress.

Glory be to the Father.

Hymn

He turned and looked on me a moment, then

There was a look of love,

Like that I saw in Pilate's hall,

When sorrowing Peter came.

Gethsemani

Eyes of Jesus, turned so tenderly upon Peter, look upon our sinful souls.

Eyes of Jesus, so expressive of the incomprehensible love of God, give us tears of repentance. Eyes beaming with encouragement to those who walk in your light, have compassion on the sinners for whom we pray.

Enlighten their minds; consume in them all that is not worthy of the heart of Jesus.

Lord, I will seek Thy Face, and I will dwell in its presence.

With Thine own divine hands engrave on my heart the word, REPARATION.

Ant. AS BLASPHEMIES COVER THE EARTH, SO MUST YOUR REPARATION BE SEEN AND KNOWN OF MEN.

V. Woe unto them who make not this reparation.

R. O all ye who would bring joy to the Face of Jesus, He asks of us the souls of our brethren who offend Him. Let us go with Him, if need be, to suffering and to death to save them.

V. Let us show our love by sacrifice.

R. The life of sacrifice for God is the only true life.

Let us Pray

Eternal Father, I offer Thee the most Holy Face of Jesus to appease Thy just wrath. Look on His wounds. Behold His humiliations. They are a meet offering to the glory of Thy holy Name, and a worthy reparation for our crimes. Eternal Father, I offer Thee the most Holy Face of Jesus in payment of my debt to the divine justice. It is the coin of infinite value which bears the image and superscription of the King of kings. Remember Thy promises to Thy divine Son, and have mercy on us. Amen.

V. Their throats are an open sepulchre. On their lips is the venom of asps.

R. Blasphemies against the divine mysteries fall like the spittle of the Jews on the Face of Jesus Christ.

V. My Lord has looked upon me, and though I have offended Him through weakness, I have wept for my faults through love.

R. I am but a sterile earth where tares and noxious weeds abound.

V. But one glance from Jesus can make the desert to blossom as the rose. He can make my penitent heart to bring forth fruit unto life eternal.

R. May the souls of the faithful departed through the mercy of God rest in peace. Amen.

WEDNESDAY

LAUDS

V. His mighty Name shall be our shield.

R. And His adorable Face shall be our fortress.

Glory be to the Father

Hymn

O gift of gifts! O grace of faith!

My God how can it be

That Thou, who hast discerning love,

Shouldst give that gift to me?

How many hearts Thou mightst have had,

More innocent than mine!

How many souls more worthy far
Of that sweet touch of Thine!

Faber

Pride has dethroned faith, and He who would have been the Liberator of the world, is rejected.

Thou hast given to man his intellect, and he has used it to defy Thee and to lead souls to ruin. Deign to preserve the pure in heart and turn aside the waters of corruption from the innocent. Lord, curse not the poisoned spring, but purify it with the salt of divine wisdom. The ocean of Thy goodness shall swallow up the waves of the troubled sea and transform them into clear and tranquil waters, reflecting the beauty of Thy Face.

My God, my hope is in Thy mercy. Our hymns shall go up to Thee as prayers and supplications for those who outrage Thee. We offer them to Thee. Do with them according to Thy love.

Ant. I HAVE LOOKED UPON THE EARTH.

V. LOVE ME AND FEAR NOTHING.

R. In the intensity of my love I will cry out with the apostle, "I could. wish myself to be anathema from Christ for my brethren."

V. Let us show our love by sacrifice.

R. The life of sacrifice for God is the only true life.

Let us pray.

Eternal Father, I offer Thee the most Holy Face of Jesus to appease Thy just wrath. Look on His wounds. Behold His humiliations. They are a meet offering to the glory of Thy holy Name, and a worthy reparation for our crimes. Eternal Father, I offer Thee the most Holy Face of Jesus in payment of my debt to the divine justice. It is the coin of infinite value which bears the image and superscription of the King of kings. Remember Thy promises to Thy divine Son, and have mercy on us. Amen.

V. Their throats are an open sepulchre. On their lips is the venom of asps.

R. Blasphemies against the divine mysteries fall like the spittle of the Jews on the Face of Jesus Christ.

V. My Lord has looked upon me, and though I have offended Him through weakness, I have wept for my faults through love.

R. I am but a sterile earth where tares and noxious weeds abound.

V. But one glance from Jesus can make the desert to blossom as the rose. He can make my penitent heart to bring forth fruit unto life eternal.

R. May the souls of the faithful departed through the mercy of God rest in peace. Amen.

WEDNESDAY

PRIME

V. His mighty Name shall be our shield.
R. And His adorable Face shall be our fortress.
Glory be to the Father.

Hymn

How will they live, how will they die,
How bear the cross of grief,
They who have not the light of faith,
The courage of belief?

The crowd of cares, the weightiest cross,
Seem trifles less than light,

> Earth looks so little and so low
> When faith shines full and bright.
>
> *Faber*

Alas, my Jesus, all vices are glorified and Thou art rejected, Thou who art the glory of Thy people Israel and the eternal salvation of souls! The book of our meditation shall be the beloved Face of Jesus, wherein are written His sorrows and His love. Here we shall find light for the mind, strength for the will, the kindling of our desires, and the end and aim toward which should tend all our labors.

Love tends upward, and will not be detained by things of earth. It seeks "Jesus who was crucified." Be humble and peaceable, and Jesus will be with thee.

V. Our Jesus is meek and humble of Heart; He loves sinners with a love strong as death. Let us love them as He does.

R. The work of reparation is the rainbow of the mercy of God. Blessed be our most compassionate Jesus!

V. Let us show our love by sacrifice.

R. The life of sacrifice for God is the only true life.

Let us pray.

Eternal Father, I offer Thee the most Holy Face of Jesus to appease Thy just wrath. Look on His wounds. Behold His humiliations. They are a meet offering to the glory of Thy holy Name, and a worthy reparation for our crimes. Eternal Father, I offer Thee the most Holy Face of Jesus in payment of my debt to the divine justice. It is the coin of infinite value which bears the image and superscription of the King of kings. Remember Thy promises to Thy divine Son, and have mercy on us. Amen.

V. Their throats are an open sepulchre. On their lips is the venom of asps.

R. Blasphemies against the divine mysteries fall like the spittle of the

Jews on the Face of Jesus Christ.

V. My Lord has looked upon me, and though I have offended Him through weakness, I have wept for my faults through love.

R. I am but a sterile earth where tares and noxious weeds abound.

V. But one glance from Jesus can make the desert to blossom as the rose. He can make my penitent heart to bring forth fruit unto life eternal.

R. May the souls of the faithful departed through the mercy of God rest in peace. Amen.

WEDNESDAY

TIERCE

V. His mighty Name shall be our shield.

R. And His adorable Face shall be our fortress.

Glory be to the Father.

Hymn

Blest is the faith divine and strong,

Of thanks and praise an endless fountain,

Whose life is one perpetual song,

High up the Saviour's holy mountain.

O Sion's songs are sweet to sing,

With melodies of gladness laden,

> Hark how the harps of angels ring,
> Hail, Son of Man! Hail, Mother-Maiden!

Rawes

Preserve us, Lord, from the sin of Pilate, from seeking favor from the enemies of God.

The people cry with deicidal hatred, "Away with Him! Crucify Him!" But like the daughters of Jerusalem, we follow Thy dear footsteps, even though it be to Calvary. O Almighty God, take not away from us the favor of Him who was the friend of sinners! Let riot that wounded Face be turned from us! Let not our self-indulgence and our unmortified life cause the bleeding Face of Jesus to be turned away from us in displeasure! Stay with us, O most compassionate, most generous, most merciful Saviour! Thy Face shall be the oriflamme that leads the way to heaven.

V. Let us show our love by sacrifice.

R. The life of sacrifice for God is the only true life.

Let us pray.

Eternal Father, I offer Thee the most Holy Face of Jesus to appease Thy just wrath. Look on His wounds. Behold His humiliations. They are a meet offering to the glory of Thy holy Name, and a worthy reparation for our crimes. Eternal Father, I offer Thee the most Holy Face of Jesus in payment of my debt to the divine justice. It is the coin of infinite value which bears the image and superscription of the King of kings. Remember Thy promises to Thy divine Son, and have mercy on us. Amen.

V. Their throats are an open sepulchre. On their lips is the venom of asps.

R. Blasphemies against the divine mysteries fall like the spittle of the Jews on the Face of Jesus Christ.

V. My Lord has looked upon me, and though I have offended Him through weakness, I have wept for my faults through love.

R. I am but a sterile earth where tares and noxious weeds abound.

V. But one glance from Jesus can make the desert to blossom as the rose. He can make my penitent heart to bring forth fruit unto life eternal.

R. May the souls of the faithful departed through the mercy of God rest in peace. Amen.

WEDNESDAY

SEXT

V. His mighty Name shall be bur shield.
R. And His adorable Face shall be our fortress.
Glory be to the Father.

Hymn

Through toils and dangers pressing cn,
As through a fiery flood,
Two slender feet beside mine own
Mark every step with blood;
The swollen veins so rent with nails,
It breaks my heart to see,
While the same sad voice cries out afresh:

> "These feet were pierced for thee!"
>
> For me, dear Christ, for me?
>
> "Yea, even so, rebellious flesh!
>
> These feet were pierced for thee!"
>
> *E. C. Donnelly*

Him, Who is the eternal Wisdom. Herod clothed with a white robe, the dress of a fool. Saviour, put me in Thy place, for I have thought and spoken like the world, and I have taken part in its folly. Lord, Thou dost direct the world by the hand of Thy justice. Make me know it, make me love it; above all, make me submit to it, indifferent to the praise or blame of the world, and let the day come when it shall reign upon the earth as it reigns in heaven.

Ant. OH, IF YOU KNEW WHAT I HAVE DONE FOR YOU, AND HOW I HAVE WATCHED OVER YOUR SOUL, YOU WOULD BE LOST IN ASTONISHMENT TO SEE THE CREATOR THUS MINDFUL OF THE CREATURE!

V. What have I to fear from the world while I have Jesus for my friend? If I possess Him, what, have I to ask of creatures?

R. The love that has taken me from nothing will raise me to heaven.

V. Let us show our love by sacrifice.

R. The life of sacrifice for God is the only true life.

Let us pray.

Eternal Father, I offer Thee the most Holy Face of Jesus to appease Thy just wrath. Look on His wounds. Behold His humiliations. They are a meet offering to the glory of Thy holy Name, and a worthy reparation for our crimes. Eternal Father, I offer Thee the most Holy Face of Jesus in payment of my debt to the divine justice. It is the coin of infinite value which bears the image and superscription of the King of kings. Remember Thy promises to Thy divine Son, and have mercy on us. Amen.

V. Their throats are an open sepulchre. On their lips is the venom of asps.

R. Blasphemies against the divine mysteries fall like the spittle of the Jews on the Face of Jesus Christ.

V. My Lord has looked upon me, and though I have offended Him through weakness, I have wept for my faults through love.

R. I am but a sterile earth where tares and noxious weeds abound.

V. But one glance from Jesus can make the desert to blossom as the rose. He can make my penitent heart to bring forth fruit unto life eternal.

R. May the souls of the faithful departed through the mercy of God rest in peace. Amen.

Wednesday

None

V. His mighty Name shall be our shield.

R. And His adorable Face shall be our fortress.

Glory be to the Father.

Hymn

The little life I had seemed lost in Him,

And pangs of superhuman pain were blinding every sense.

Yet there in all the awful night.

My blessed love was nigh.

And I was watching Him,

And if my tears were flowing fast,

My weeping was for Him.

Gethsemani

"Then Pilate took Jesus and scourged Him." Pilate? Nay, but we. We have done it by our sensuality, our worldliness, our love of ease. Even His blessed feet were torn and bleeding that the sins of our feet, walking in the paths of wickedness, might be expiated. Even His holy hands were struck and wounded that He might atone for the sins of our hands in all our evil works. The adorable Face of Jesus was marred more than man, because in our faces have flamed the baleful fires of pride, anger, and every evil passion. Let me take my place beside my God, outraged and despised. What other glory shall I seek but that of likeness to Jesus crucified?

Ant. "IF YOU ARE UNFAITHFUL TO MY VOICE, YOU SHALL FEEL IN YOURSELF THE BLOWS OF THE SCOURGE. STRIVE TO TAKE IT FROM MY HAND.

V. IF BY YOUR FAULT MY DESIGNS ARE THWARTED, I WILL HOLD YOU ACCOUNTABLE FOR SOULS.

R. O infinite goodness of my God, help me to pray, to speak, that Thou mayest be more and more known and loved!

V. Let us show our love by sacrifice.

R. The life of sacrifice for God is the only true life.

Let us pray.

Eternal Father, I offer Thee the most Holy Face of Jesus to appease Thy just wrath. Look on His wounds. Behold His humiliations. They are a meet offering to the glory of Thy holy Name, and a worthy reparation for our crimes. Eternal Father, I offer Thee the most Holy Face of Jesus in payment of my debt to the divine justice. It is the coin of infinite value which bears the image and superscription of the King of kings. Remember Thy promises to Thy divine Son, and have mercy on us. Amen.

V. Their throats are an open sepulchre. On their lips is the venom of asps.

R. Blasphemies against the divine mysteries fall like the spittle of the Jews on the Face of Jesus Christ.

V. My Lord has looked upon me, and though I have offended Him through weakness, I have wept for my faults through love.

R. I am but a sterile earth where tares and noxious weeds abound.

V. But one glance from Jesus can make the desert to blossom as the rose. He can make my penitent heart to bring forth fruit unto life eternal.

R. May the souls of the faithful departed through the mercy of God rest in peace. Amen.

WEDNESDAY

VESPERS

V. His mighty Name shall be our shield.

R. And His adorable Face shall be our fortress.

Glory be to the Father.

Hymn

The waters of remorse engulfed my soul.

Each infidelity of all my life,

Each act or word wherein I had denied

The heavenly Bridegroom dear,

To whom I plighted all my heart,—all came before me now.

I saw them in my Master's Face, I read them in His tears.

Gethsemani

Falsehood is the king of this world. Truth walks barefooted and despised, like Jesus Christ. O eternal Truth, we take Thee for the companion of our pilgrimage. He who Brought light to the human race is struck by servants!

Science accuses Him, history denies Him, and the satanic genius of man strikes His august Face.

O Face of my adored Master, behold our affliction and help us in our resolution to be true to those virtues which are most opposed to the vices of the day!

Ant. In proportion to your spirit of reparation, I will impress My image upon you and make you beautiful as you were, when, at the baptismal font, you were made stainless and pure.

V. We are the happy flock of which Jesus is the divine Shepherd.

R. We will go with Him to seek the lost sheep, and His grief for them shall find comfort in our zeal.

V. Let us show our love by sacrifice.

R. The life of sacrifice for God is the only true life.

Let us pray.

Eternal Father, I offer Thee the most Holy Face of Jesus to appease Thy just wrath. Look on His wounds. Behold His humiliations. They are a meet offering to the glory of Thy holy Name, and a worthy reparation for our crimes. Eternal Father, I offer Thee the most Holy Face of Jesus in payment of my debt to the divine justice. It is the coin of infinite value which bears the image and superscription of the King of kings. Remember Thy promises to Thy divine Son, and have mercy on us. Amen.

V. Their throats are an open sepulchre. On their lips is the venom of asps.

R. Blasphemies against the divine mysteries fall like the spittle of the Jews on the Face of Jesus Christ.

V. My Lord has looked upon me, and though I have offended Him through weakness, I have wept for my faults through love.

R. I am but a sterile earth where tares and noxious weeds abound.

V. But one glance from Jesus can make the desert to blossom as the rose. He can make my penitent heart to bring forth fruit unto life eternal.

R. May the souls of the faithful departed through the mercy of God rest in peace. Amen.

WEDNESDAY

COMPLINE

V. His mighty Name shall be our shield.

R. And His adorable Face shall be our fortress.

Glory be to the Father.

O Master dear, my King, I cried,

Show me Thy Face once more.

O tell me, is Thy trial ended now?

Coarse voices shouted long and loud:

"Let Him be crucified!" "Let Caesar's rival die!"

Gethsemani

O my sweet Saviour, I die of shame and remorse; for I, too, have
preferred Barabbas to Jesus, sin to holiness, deformity to divine

beauty. I have taken part with the executioners and have merited eternal damnation.

I bury myself in my nothingness; but Jesus loves the poor in spirit and turns from the proud. Pour forth upon us, O compassionate Saviour, upon us who have nothing, and who are nothing, the infinite treasures of Thy love!

Ant. I to my Beloved and my Beloved to me.

V. Let us show our love by sacrifice.

R. The life of sacrifice for God is the only true life.

Let us pray.

Eternal Father, I offer Thee the most Holy Face of Jesus to appease Thy just wrath. Look on His wounds. Behold His humiliations. They are a meet offering to the glory of Thy holy Name, and a worthy reparation for our crimes. Eternal Father, I offer Thee the most Holy Face of Jesus in payment of my debt to the divine justice. It is the coin of infinite value which bears the image and superscription of the King of kings. Remember Thy promises to Thy divine Son, and have mercy on us. Amen.

V. Their throats are an open sepulchre. On their lips is the venom of asps.

R. Blasphemies against the divine mysteries fall like the spittle of the Jews on the Face of Jesus Christ.

V. My Lord has looked upon me, and though I have offended Him through weakness, I have wept for my faults through love.

R. I am but a sterile earth where tares and noxious weeds abound.

V. But one glance from Jesus can make the desert to blossom as the rose. He can make my penitent heart to bring forth fruit unto life eternal.

R. May the souls of the faithful departed through the mercy of God rest in peace. Amen.

Prayer.

O Jesus, Thou art surely God to bear with us and dwell so patiently among us. How few there are who have the courage to range themselves under Thy standard and do battle with those who lead Thee again to Calvary!

As in the days of Thy passion. Thou art alone in the hands. of Thine enemies. Alas, if we have not the gift of tears like St. Peter, at least let us beat our breasts with the multitude returning to Jerusalem and acknowledging that "indeed this was the Son of God." O Holy Spirit, enliven us, and give us courage to throw ourselves in the vanguard of the strife. Give us the victory, and let all hearts own Thee for their king.

V. Adorable Jesus, teach us to compassionate Thy sufferings on earth, that we may merit to have a share in Thy glory in heaven.
R. This Face so marred and bruised shall one day appear, radiant in glory, and its enemies shall be annihilated forever.

V. The spirits of evil shall be driven back into darkness, and the Holy Face shall reign upon earth.

Blessed art thou, O Israel. Who is like unto thee, O people that art saved by the Lord, the shield of thy help, the sword of thy glory! Thine enemies shall deny thee and thou shalt tread upon their necks.

Lord, let us walk in the light of Thy Face, and rejoice day and night in the praise of Thy Name.

V. May the souls of the faithful departed through the mercy of God rest in peace.

R. And may the chains be broken that hold them captive far from Thy Face. Amen.

THURSDAY

MATINS

Hail Mary.

O Jesus, Thou hast promised all good gifts to those who adore Thy Holy Face in reparation for blasphemies uttered against Thy holy Name and the teachings of Thy Church.

Offer to the eternal Father, we implore Thee, these prayers which we pour forth for the greater glory of God and the conversion of sinners.

Our Father, who art in heaven, look not upon us only, but upon the Face of Thy Christ.

V. O Lord, show us Thy face, and we shall be saved.

R. Turn Thy Face towards us, and give us peace.

V. His mighty Name shall be our shield.

R. And His adorable Face shall be our fortress.

Glory be to the Father.

Hymn

I heard the Roman say: "Behold the Man!"

Then while I looked and loved,

As I had never loved before, I seemed to catch

The notes of some celestial song,

Which, far above the sinful noise of earth,

Was sounding in the skies.

"Indeed, behold the Man, the Virgin's child,

The Word made flesh, the Adam of the new and living face.

All worthy, is the Lamb that dies.

This is the Son of God. Sing, ye choirs of spirits blest,

Come sing His everlasting reign!"

Gethsemani

Jesus, Thou art the splendor of the Father. I gaze upon Thine outraged Face, where, even beneath the veil of blood, Thy Divinity shines forth.

O Sovereign Majesty, enduring such pain and shame at the hands of Thy creatures, raise up an army of penitents to form a guard of honor before Thy Holy Face. Raise up a multitude of souls, from whose loving hearts shall ascend a perpetual homage of reparation and praise.

Ant. I WOULD HAVE YOU LITTLE, WITH A GREAT HEART.

V. It is the glory of the just to do Thy will.

R. O blessed Face, source of light, transfigure them who contemplate Thee. But let not our adoration be sterile. We offer Thee the incense of loving fear and obedient love.

V. Save, O Lord, save Thy people.

R. And be not angry with us forever.

Let us Pray

O Jesus, cast upon us a look of mercy; turn Thy Face toward each one of us, as Thou didst turn it to Veronica. Not that we may see it with our mortal eyes: this we are not worthy of; but turn it to our hearts, that so, drawn *to* Thee, we may draw *from* Thee strength and vigor for the combat of this life.[1]

V. And He was as a leper and as one struck by God and afflicted.

R. Poverty is the school of patience.

V. Let us embrace it with love, and abandon ourselves to the guidance of God.

R. May the souls of the faithful departed through the mercy of God rest in peace. Amen.

---

1. Pope Pius IX.

Thursday

Lauds

V. His mighty Name shall be our shield.

R. And His adorable Face shall be our fortress.

Glory be to the Father.

Hymn

I saw my Jesus standing in the court.

The sad procession stays a moment there.

Dread silence reigns where curse and jeer

Were sounding in the air. They bring the heavy cross,

The sacred wood for which He sighed,

The blessed tree that bears the fruit of life.

Alas! its awful weight

Will crush His wasted frame.

It is His burden dear;

The sins of all the world are resting there.

With rudeness vile, with cruel haste,

They lay it on His shoulders, gashed and bleeding from the scourge.

He staggers helplessly.

He trembles fearfully.

His blessed Face turns icy pale.

He gasps for breath. He nearly falls.

He moves with pain.

His Face is like the face of death.

Gethsemani

No, no more sin to crush the tender Heart of Jesus. No more sin to bruise the blessed Face of my Redeemer.

Let me live a new life, a life of reparation, a life of humility, a life lost in God.

Ant. I WILL GIVE THEE MY FACE IN THE PRESENCE OF MY FATHER, IN THE POWER OF THE HOLY GHOST, AND BEFORE THE WHOLE COURT OF HEAVEN.

V. MY HOLY MOTHER AND ST. VERONICA SHALL SHOW IT TO YOU, AND THEY WILL TEACH YOU TO VENERATE IT.

R. In the name of Veronica's act of compassion, give, O Lord, to sinners perfect contrition at the hour of their death.

V. Save, O Lord, save Thy people.

R. And be not angry with us forever.

Let us pray.

O Jesus, cast upon us a look of mercy; turn Thy Face toward each one of us, as Thou didst turn it to Veronica. Not that we may see it with our mortal eyes: this we are not worthy of; but turn it to our hearts, that so, drawn *to* Thee, we may draw *from* Thee strength and vigor for the combat of this life.

V. And He was as a leper and as one struck by God and afflicted.

R. Poverty is the school of patience.

V. Let us embrace it with love, and abandon ourselves to the guidance of God.

R. May the souls of the faithful departed through the mercy of God rest in peace. Amen.

Thursday

Prime

V. His mighty Name shall be our shield.

R. And His adorable Face shall be our fortress.

Glory be to the Father.

Hymn

His Face was sad and pale; His eyes were full of tears.

His precious lips were trembling as He seemed to say:

I am condemned to death. Now let Me look on thee.

Art thou indeed My spouse? Then pray for grace.

I go before thee with My staff and rod.

The clouds shall cover thee in gloom;

The waters cold shall swallow thee with Me;

The prince of earth shall reign. Yet come, My loving child!

The Bridegroom leads the sorrowing way;

The Spirit bids the bride to come.

Gethsemani

O Jesus, dearest Friend, beloved Redeemer, Thou dost ascend the hill of Calvary followed by the murderous blasphemies of Thy chosen people. Thou fallest, and there is none to aid Thee. Thy Face is torn, Thy hands are bleeding, Thou takest up the burden of the cross again, and Thou toilest on without complaint.

Let me imitate Thee. Suffering is the dead sea fruit of sin; the love of Jesus changes it into the fruit of life. Suffering is the divine ordeal.

O God of love, I will take up the burden of life again with courage and humility. To walk with Thee, to suffer with Thee, to be lost in Thee, to love as Thou dost,—is not this the happiness of earth while we wait for the happiness of heaven?

Ant. OH, IF YOU COULD BUT SEE THE BEAUTY OF MY FACE!

V. The Holy Face is the sensible object of our adoration, which, we offer for the outrages of blasphemies against God.

R. Spare, O Lord, spare Thy people, and be not angry with us forever.

Let us pray.

O Jesus, cast upon us a look of mercy; turn Thy Face toward each one of us, as Thou didst turn it to Veronica. Not that we may see it with our mortal eyes: this we are not worthy of; but turn it to our hearts, that so, drawn *to* Thee, we may draw *from* Thee strength and vigor for the combat of this life.

V. And He was as a leper and as one struck by God and afflicted.

R. Poverty is the school of patience.

V. Let us embrace it with love, and abandon ourselves to the guidance of God.

R. May the souls of the faithful departed through the mercy of God rest in peace. Amen.

Thursday

Tierce

V. His mighty Name shall be our shield.

R. And His adorable Face shall be our fortress.

Glory be to the Father.

Hymn

And now you hear the blessed name of the Immaculate:

Go meet her as she comes;

Go pray to her for grace to know

The riches of the Heart

That calleth you from every tie;

Go kneel where she shall kneel,

Go look upon her blessed face,

And put your hand in hers.

Gethsemani

O Mother most afflicted, thy holy tears break my heart! I have caused thy grief, I have crucified thy Son. My infidelities, my pride, my unmortified spirit, my sensuality have loaded Him with their heavy weight so that He has fallen by the way. But I renounce them and I would atone for them. O Mother, the victim of ungrateful hearts, obtain for me the true spirit of penance.

Ant. THE HOLY NAME OF GOD EXPRESSES THE DIVINITY AND CONTAINS WITHIN IT ALL THE PERFECTION OF THE CREATOR.

V. Save, O Lord, save Thy people.

R. And be not angry with us forever.

Let us pray.

O Jesus, cast upon us a look of mercy; turn Thy Face toward each one of us, as Thou didst turn it to Veronica. Not that we may see it with our mortal eyes: this we are not worthy of; but turn it to our hearts, that so, drawn *to* Thee, we may draw *from* Thee strength and vigor for the combat of this life.

V. And He was as a leper and as one struck by God and afflicted.

R. Poverty is the school of patience.

V. Let us embrace it with love, and abandon ourselves to the guidance of God.

R. May the souls of the faithful departed through the mercy of God rest in peace. Amen.

THURSDAY

SEXT

V. His holy Name shall be our shield.

R. And His Holy Face shall be our fortress.

Glory be to the Father.

Hymn

See, here the holy woman comes to me;

She beareth here the awful picture of my Child.

Oh! let us look upon that Face so bruised and torn.

See here the gashes of the thorns, the marks of clotted blood,

The courses of the tears.

Behold the anguish of that brow!—O precious Face!

I know it well! I know its every line!

Gethsemani

Blessed Veronica, fain would I share with you the tender ministry oh the road to Calvary. Happy woman, to have been permitted to prove your love, and brave the hatred of the rabble. To you it was given to refresh and soothe the suffering, sorrowful Face of Jesus in His Passion.

But not to you alone. I too am called to follow in your generous footsteps. Blasphemies are poured out like defilement upon the Holy Face of Jesus. If I suffer with Him for the guilty, I too comfort the beloved Face and call down pardon upon those who offend Him.

Happy Veronica, so reverently preserving the veil which had touched the adorable features of our Beloved! A copy of this treasure is mine; I will wear it on my heart, and nothing shall draw me from its contemplation.

Ant. I SEEK VERONICAS TO HONOR MY DIVINE FACE. IT'S ADORERS ARE FEW.

V. ALL WHO EMBRACE THIS DEVOTION, COMPASSIONATE ME, WITH VERONICA, ON THE WAY TO CALVARY.

V. Save, O Lord, save Thy people.

R. And be not angry with us forever.

Let us pray.

O Jesus, cast upon us a look of mercy; turn Thy Face toward each one of us, as Thou didst turn it to Veronica. Not that we may see it with our mortal eyes: this we are not worthy of; but turn it to our hearts, that so, drawn *to* Thee, we may draw *from* Thee strength and vigor for the combat of this life.

V. And He was as a leper and as one struck by God and afflicted.

R. Poverty is the school of patience.

V. Let us embrace it with love, and abandon ourselves to the guidance of God.

R. May the souls of the faithful departed through the mercy of God rest in peace. Amen.

Thursday

None

V. His holy Name shall be our shield.

R. And His adorable Face shall be our fortress.

Glory be to the Father.

Hymn

Dear Lord, admit me to Thy sanctuary;
The dawn shines through Thy door.
And oh! the night has been so wild and weary;
Say, shall I wander more?
Oh, let me in to shelter everlasting!
I weep against Thy door.

For hope of rest my weary soul is wasting;

Say, shall I wander more?

R. M.

Hail! Holy Face of our Redeemer, in which is reflected the splendor of God. Imprinted upon a veil of snowy whiteness Thou didst give it to Veronica as a sign of love. Hail! treasure of the world, joy of the saints, the desired of hearts that love Thee. Purify us from all spot of stain, and admit us to the company of the blessed. We have wandered, we have not loved Thee, we have eaten of the husks of the world. Worn and weary, we return to our Father's house, and would never more go out therefrom.

Ant. LOVE SHALL WIPE THE BLOODSTAINS FROM MY FACE.

V. ALL THAT A SOUL DOES FOR MY GLORY IS A CONSOLATION UNSPEAKABLE TO MY HEART.

R. To glorify Thee! To love Thee! O Jesus, how shall I be worthy of so glorious a vocation? Grant that I may persevere in this path of reparation and salvation, in which Thy grace has placed my feet.

V. Save, O Lord, save Thy people.

R. And be not angry with us forever.

Let us pray.

O Jesus, cast upon us a look of mercy; turn Thy Face toward each one of us, as Thou didst turn it to Veronica. Not that we may see it with our mortal eyes: this we are not worthy of; but turn it to our hearts, that so, drawn *to* Thee, we may draw *from* Thee strength and vigor for the combat of this life.

V. And He was as a leper and as one struck by God and afflicted.

R. Poverty is the school of patience.

V. Let us embrace it with love, and abandon ourselves to the guidance of God.

R. May the souls of the faithful departed through the mercy of God rest in peace. Amen.

THURSDAY

VESPERS

V. His holy Name shall be our shield.

R. And His adorable Face shall be our fortress.

Glory be to the Father.

Hymn

I pass beneath the shadow of Thy woe,

And all Thy mighty sorrow comes to me;

A blinding agony that none can know,

A brooding desolation like the sea.

Heavy and lurid hangs the gathering storm.

I pass beneath the shadow of Thy pain;

Beneath the olives lies a prostrate form,

And on their roots there falls a warm, red rain,

Rawes

Those who bear the cross of Jesus shall want for nothing, for love is its own reward.

To know the mystery and beauty of the cross, we must stretch ourselves upon that wood of sacrifice with Jesus. Before we can taste the sweets of pure love, we must tear out of our hearts all attachments to creatures. We must break with all that is the enemy of the poverty of Jesus; we must tear down and root up before we can build upon the divine foundation, which is the cross of Christ.

Ant. ASK OF MY FATHER AS MANY SOULS AS I HAVE SHED DROPS OF BLOOD IN MY PASSION.

Ant. WHEN YOU MAKE AN ACT OF LOVE TO ME, I TAKE YOUR HEART IN My HANDS, AND I WILL KEEP IT SAFE.

R. Lord, make me what Thou wilt, and use my whole being in Thy service.

V. Save, O Lord, save Thy people.

R. And be not angry with us forever.

Let us pray.

O Jesus, cast upon us a look of mercy; turn Thy Face toward each one of us, as Thou didst turn it to Veronica. Not that we may see it with our mortal eyes: this we are not worthy of; but turn it to our hearts, that so, drawn *to* Thee, we may draw *from* Thee strength and vigor for the combat of this life.

V. And He was as a leper and as one struck by God and afflicted.

R. Poverty is the school of patience.

V. Let us embrace it with love, and abandon ourselves to the guidance of God.

R. May the souls of the faithful departed through the mercy of God rest in peace. Amen.

Thursday

Compline

V. His mighty Name shall be our shield.

R. And His adorable Face shall be our fortress.

Glory be to the Father.

Hymn

I hear the scourges in the cold night air,

I see the thorns around Thy throbbing head;

Then dost Thou find no answer to Thy prayer,

And on the ground Thy tears and blood are shed.

Why is Thy raiment red?

Why is it Thou dost come

In such a guise from Bosra? One replied:
The sinless Victim bears the sinner's doom.

Rawes

I am the cause of Thy martyrdom, O bleeding Lamb of God! Thou dost willingly yield Thy members to the executioners, and I reject the cross Thy mercy has formed for me.

Henceforth, dear Jesus, I will embrace it, be it formed of sufferings of body or of mind, of heart-rending separations, or of poverty; let it come with lingering pain, a long-foreseen anguish, or let it crush me to the earth with a sudden blow; I will stretch myself upon the Cross with Thee, O my most compassionate Jesus.

With this sacred cross I will knock at the door of heaven, and it shall open to me a blessed eternity.

Ant. I WILL GIVE YOU MY HOLY FACE AS A REWARD FOR ALL YOUR LABORS IN MY CAUSE.

V. BY MY HOLY FACE YOU WILL OBTAIN THE CONVERSION OF MANY SINNERS.

R. Dear Jesus, I offer Thee Thy Holy Face, and I pray with the Psalmist: Have mercy on them, O Lord, according to Thy great mercy, and according to the multitude of Thy tender mercies blot out their iniquity. Wash them yet more from their iniquity, and cleanse them from their sin.

V. Save, O Lord, save Thy people,

R. And be not angry with us forever.

Let us pray.

O Jesus, cast upon us a look of mercy; turn Thy Face toward each one of us, as Thou didst turn it to Veronica. Not that we may see it with our mortal eyes: this we are not worthy of; but turn it to our hearts, that so, drawn *to* Thee, we may draw *from* Thee strength and vigor for the combat of this life.

V. And He was as a leper and as one struck by God and afflicted.

R. Poverty is the school of patience.

V. Let us embrace it with love, and abandon ourselves to the guidance of God.

R. May the souls of the faithful departed through the mercy of God rest in peace. Amen.

Prayer.

O Jesus, Thou art surely God to bear with us and dwell so patiently among us. How few there are who have the courage to range themselves under Thy standard and do battle with those who lead Thee again to Calvary!

As in the days of Thy passion. Thou art alone in the hands of Thine enemies. Alas, if we have not the gift of tears like St. Peter, at least let us beat our breasts with the multitude returning to Jerusalem and acknowledging that "indeed this was the Son of God." O Holy Spirit, enliven us, and give us courage to throw ourselves in the vanguard of the strife. Give us the victory, and let all hearts own Thee for their king.

V. Adorable Jesus, teach us to compassionate Thy sufferings on earth, that we may merit to have a share in Thy glory in heaven.

R. This Face so marred and bruised shall one day appear, radiant in glory, and its enemies shall be annihilated forever.

V. The spirits of evil shall be driven back into darkness, and the Holy Face shall reign upon earth.

Blessed art thou, O Israel. Who is like unto thee, O people that art saved by the Lord, the shield of thy help, the sword of thy glory! Thine enemies shall deny thee and thou shalt tread upon their necks.

Lord, let us walk in the light of Thy Face, and rejoice day and night in the praise of Thy Name.

V. May the souls of the faithful departed through the mercy of God rest in peace.

R. And may the chains be broken that hold them captive far from Thy Face. Amen.

FRIDAY

MATINS

Hail Mary.

O Jesus, Thou hast promised all good gifts to those who adore Thy Holy Face in reparation for blasphemies, uttered against Thy holy Name and the teachings of Thy Church.

Offer to the eternal Father, we implore Thee, these prayers which we pour forth for the greater glory of God and the conversion of sinners.

Our Father who art in heaven, look not upon us only, but upon the Face of Thy Christ.

> *V.* O Lord, show us Thy Face, and we shall be saved.
>
> *R.* Turn Thy Face toward us, and give us peace.

V. His mighty Name shall be our shield.

R. And His adorable Face shall be our fortress.

Glory be to the Father..

Hymn

Dark, nameless anguish doth upon Thee lie,

Dark woe with dim, oppressive pain;

Fever of burning thirst, an agony

Not known before and never known again.

So do I search along the thorn-strewn way,

But other grief like Thine I cannot see;

And through the storm I seem to hear Thee say,

A vintage now the Lord hath made of Me.

Rawes

O divine Martyr of love, there is an expression in Thy blessed Face that Comes not from the anguish of the nails. There are shame and grief: grief for the sinner arid shame for the sin.

Thou art meek, my Jesus, and Thou art led like a lamb, submitting unresistingly to the will of the mob, thirsting for Thy blood. Thou art humble, and Thou seest in our salvation the triumph of the Eternal Father.

Thou art obedient unto death, even the death of the cross. Deliver me from all desire of being praised, sought after, or loved. Thee only, my Saviour; God alone, in life and in death.

Ant. TAKE COMFORT, MY CHILD; I GO BEFORE THEE IN THE WAY OF THE CROSS. THE NAILS WILL PIERCE MY FLESH BEFORE THEY COME TO THEE.

R. Dear Master, may they nail me to the cross beside Thee, and may I taste of this divine intimacy with my God.

V. The Sacred Heart is the place of my rest.

R. Here will I dwell, for I have chosen it.

Let us Pray

O Saviour Jesus, at the sight of Thy Holy Face so disfigured by sorrow, at the sight of Thy Sacred Heart so full of love, I cry out with St. Augustine: Write, I beseech Thee, O Lord, Thy wounds upon my heart, that I may read therein sorrow and love; sorrow to, endure every sorrow for Thee, and love to despise every love for Thee.

V. O Face so full of compassion, by the sacred blood streaming from Thee,

R. By Thy divine humiliations and Thy glorious martyrdom,

V. Be the Redeemer of sinners.

R. O Jesus, save the world.

V. We will grasp Thy bleeding cross and bear it on our hearts.

R. May the souls of the faithful departed through the mercy of God rest in peace.

Friday

Lauds

V. His holy Name shall be our shield.

R. And His adorable Face shall be our fortress.

Glory be to the Father.

Hymn

I pass beneath the shadow of Thy woe,

The dark, strong anguish of Thy Sacred Heart,

I long to bear it with me where I go,

That I from Thee may never more depart.

Darkly there hangs above me on my way

This world-wide, world-deep agony of Thine;

With me, dear Lord, forever may there stay

This shadow of an agony divine.

Rawes

Hail, majestic Face, raised between earth and heaven!

Face of my God, enlighten me.

Face of my Father, direct me.

Face of my Master, instruct me.

Face of my Friend, comfort me.

Face of my Judge, have compassion upon me.

Face of my Brother, pay my debt to the divine justice.

Face of my King, reign forever oyer a purified world.

Face of my Redeemer, may all hearts bless and adore Thee, and sacrifice themselves for Thy glory.

Ant. I WILL SUFFER IN YOU TO APPEASE THE ANGER OF MY FATHER.

V. I WILL GIVE YOU ALL MY MERITS WHEREWITH TO PAY YOUR DEBTS.

R. Jesus stands between sinners and the Eternal Father. The outrages which cannot reach the Father fall in ignominious showers upon the divine Face.

V. The Sacred Heart is the place of my rest.

R. Here will I dwell, for I have chosen it.

Let us pray.

O Saviour Jesus, at the sight of Thy Holy Face so disfigured by sorrow, at the sight of Thy Sacred Heart so full of love, I cry out with St. Augustine: Write, I beseech Thee, O Lord, Thy wounds upon my heart, that I may read therein sorrow and love; sorrow to, endure every sorrow for Thee, and love to despise every love for Thee.

V. O Face so full of compassion, by the sacred blood streaming from Thee,

R. By Thy divine humiliations and Thy glorious martyrdom,

V. Be the Redeemer of sinners.

R. O Jesus, save the world.

V. We will grasp Thy bleeding cross and bear it on our hearts.

R. May the souls of the faithful departed through the mercy of God rest in peace.

Friday

Prime

V. His holy Name shall be our shield.

R. And His adorable Face shall be our fortress.

Glory be to the Father.

Hymn

O starlit sky, pour forth thy tears;

Men turn aside from God, nor know

His beauty; weep for darkening woe,

Weep for the loveless years.

O sun and moon, be dark above;

Why shine when God is scarcely seen?

His love the same has ever been,

Yet men forget that love.

Rawes

O Jesus crucified, I adore in silence Thy Face bowed down upon the cross. Let my soul bathe in the Precious Blood which flows so abundantly for us. In this celestial bath, I would drown forever all that in me is offensive to the divine eyes.

When Thou wert treated as a criminal, how can I seek for the applause of the world! When Thy head was crowned with thorns, shall I desire to be crowned with flowers? When Thou didst take Thy rest upon the cross, how shall I give myself up to self-indulgence and sensuality!

It is all over; henceforth I will rest with Jesus; I will dwell at the foot of the cross: there is my rest forever and ever.

Ant. I HAVE TAKEN UPON ME ALL THE SINS OF THE WORLD.

V. I WILL THAT THOU TAKE UPON THEE THE SINS OF THY BRETHREN, THAT THOU MAYEST MAKE REPARATION FOR THEM.

R. So shall we bring forth souls for God.

V. The Sacred Heart is the place of my rest.

R. Here will I dwell, for I have chosen it.

Let us pray.

O Saviour Jesus, at the sight of Thy Holy Face so disfigured by sorrow, at the sight of Thy Sacred Heart so full of love, I cry out with St. Augustine: Write, I beseech Thee, O Lord, Thy wounds upon my heart, that I may read therein sorrow and love; sorrow to, endure every sorrow for Thee, and love to despise every love for Thee.

V. O Face so full of compassion, by the sacred blood streaming from Thee,

R. By Thy divine humiliations and Thy glorious martyrdom,

V. Be the Redeemer of sinners.

R. O Jesus, save the world.

V. We will grasp Thy bleeding cross and bear it on our hearts.

R. May the souls of the faithful departed through the mercy of God rest in peace.

FRIDAY

TIERCE

V. His mighty Name shall be our shield.

R. And His adorable Face shall be our fortress.

Glory be to the Father.

Hymn

Oh, turn those blessed points, all bathed
In Jesus' blood, on me;
Mine were the sins that wrought His death,
Mine be the penalty.
Pierce through my feet, my hands, my heart;
So may some drop distill

Of blood divine into my soul,
And all its evils heal.

Breviary

"Lord, remember me when Thou comest into Thy kingdom." So spake the "good thief," and love drew him from his infamy. He saw the light of heaven shining in the Holy Face, and his soul turned like a flower to the sun.

Pardon! It is a new birth, it is the realization of all our hopes for eternity! It is the sight of the well-beloved Face. Thou art condemned, O King eternal; but I know Thee who Thou art; I too see the glory of heaven shining through the abjection of the crucified humanity. I have confessed my sins, and I have done penance for them. "Now, to be Thine, yea, Thine alone, O Lamb of God, I come."

Ant. SUFFER AND PRAY.

V. BY MY FACE YOU SHALL WORK MIRACLES.

R. How shall we dare complain of suffering? Thou, my Jesus, wast crucified for ungrateful souls. But we, we are crucified for a God who will give us a hundredfold in this world and life eternal hereafter.

V. The Sacred Heart is the place of my rest.

R. Here will I dwell, for I have chosen it.

Let us pray.

O Saviour Jesus, at the sight of Thy Holy Face so disfigured by sorrow, at the sight of Thy Sacred Heart so full of love, I cry out with St. Augustine: Write, I beseech Thee, O Lord, Thy wounds upon my heart, that I may read therein sorrow and love; sorrow to, endure every sorrow for Thee, and love to despise every love for Thee.

V. O Face so full of compassion, by the sacred blood streaming from Thee,

R. By Thy divine humiliations and Thy glorious martyrdom,

V. Be the Redeemer of sinners.

R. O Jesus, save the world.

V. We will grasp Thy bleeding cross and bear it on our hearts.

R. May the souls of the faithful departed through the mercy of God rest in peace.

FRIDAY

SEXT

V. His mighty Name shall be our shield.
R. And His adorable Face shall be our fortress.
Glory be to the Father.
Hymn
Look down, O God; be near us, Lord;
The world-wide struggle cannot cease,
Not yet we win the Master's peace,
For Thou hast sent the sword.
The day is struggling with the night,
And with the good, dark evil strives.

Gladly for Thee we risk our lives,

Thou great unchanging Light.

The nations live in proud indifference to the laws of God.

We have heard, with trembling hearts, that awful blasphemy: "If He be the Son of God, let Him come down from the cross."

O Divine Saviour, Thou who shalt save Thy people from their sins, come not down from the cross, for it is our only hope. We renounce all self-seeking, and henceforth we will live and die at Thy feet, as slaves to Thy justice, content if only we can make reparation for the least of the offences against Thy love.

Ant. Be thou faithful unto death.

V. KNOW THAT IT IS GREAT VOCATION TO BE APPOINTED TO MANIFEST MY WILL.

R. O my dear Redeemer, I prefer Thee to all Thy gifts. Thy will is my law; to please Thee is my sole desire.

V. The Sacred Heart is the place of my rest.

R. Here will I dwell, for I have chosen it.

Let us pray.

O Saviour Jesus, at the sight of Thy Holy Face so disfigured by sorrow, at the sight of Thy Sacred Heart so full of love, I cry out with St. Augustine: Write, I beseech Thee, O Lord, Thy wounds upon my heart, that I may read therein sorrow and love; sorrow to, endure every sorrow for Thee, and love to despise every love for Thee.

V. O Face so full of compassion, by the sacred blood streaming from Thee,

R. By Thy divine humiliations and Thy glorious martyrdom,

V. Be the Redeemer of sinners.

R. O Jesus, save the world.

V. We will grasp Thy bleeding cross and bear it on our hearts.

R. May the souls of the faithful departed through the mercy of God rest in peace.

Friday

None

V. His holy Name shall be our shield.
R. And His adorable Face shall be our fortress.
Glory be to the Father.

Hymn

One rest for those who suffer and are weary;
One bliss for all, when life-long work is done:
The unveiled Face of Father, Son, and Spirit;
The sight, glad-making, of God Three in One.
Steep in Thy love my soul, by Thee enkindled;
Through all my heart Thyself in sweetness pour.

Thine let me be, in living and in dying;

Thine, only Thine, Beloved, evermore.

Rawes

I praise Thee, O adorable Face, for all the tender words that fell from Thy dying lips.

I venerate Thee, O compassionate Face, for the infinite tenderness with which Thou didst look upon Thy executioners.

I adore Thee, O august Face, for the gentleness with which Thou didst show Thy Mother to St. John, and didst console Thy friends.

I bless Thee, O Holy Face, worthy of all adoration, which dost submit to the outrages of the wicked, and the infidelities and indifferences of Thy servants.

By that Face, despised by men and adored by angels, forgive them, O eternal Father.

By Thy dying, agonies on the cross, give life to sinners; pardon them, O eternal Father.

To our last hour we will cry with Jesus crucified, "Father, forgive them, for they know not what they do."

Ant. OFFER YOUR WHOLE BEING TO ME, AND BE READY TO SUFFER IN BODY AND SOUL WHATSOEVER I SHALL SEND UPON YOU, FOR THE ACCOMPLISHMENT OF MY DESIGNS.

V. MY DAUGHTER, I LOVE OBEDIENCE.

R. Lord, I have nothing that is not Thine. Speak, Lord, for Thy servant heareth.

V. The Sacred Heart is the place of my rest.

R. Here will I dwell, for I have chosen it.

Let us pray.

O Saviour Jesus, at the sight of Thy Holy Face so disfigured by sorrow, at the sight of Thy Sacred Heart so full of love, I cry out with

St. Augustine: Write, I beseech Thee, O Lord, Thy wounds upon my heart, that I may read therein sorrow and love; sorrow to, endure every sorrow for Thee, and love to despise every love for Thee.

V. O Face so full of compassion, by the sacred blood streaming from Thee,

R. By Thy divine humiliations and Thy glorious martyrdom,

V. Be the Redeemer of sinners.

R. O Jesus, save the world.

V. We will grasp Thy bleeding cross and bear it on our hearts.

R. May the souls of the faithful departed through the mercy of God rest in peace.

FRIDAY

VESPERS

V. His holy Name shall be our shield.

R. And His adorable Face shall be our fortress.

Glory be to the Father.

Hymn

The sorrowing heart, in pain and grief
Still loves, nor doubts its Father's care;
Beneath the cross it finds relief,
With Jesus and His Mother there.
As every pain is meted out,
And every sorrow knows its place,

Bearing them all without a doubt.

It looks up in its Father's Face.

The soul of Jesus was sorrowful even unto death.

My Saviour, I repeat Thy cry, sweet to me as a prayer; for a cruel grief, which is to me an interior death, holds me in its grasp.

My God, my God, why hast Thou forsaken me?

Blessed Face, I seek for Thee in my sorrow. My soul is sorrowful almost unto death, and yet it is filled with the peace of God.

If I find no consolation, I feel Thy cross is in my hand, and with it for a compass, one cannot go astray. "We hold and are held."

Thy cross shall lead me to the blessed land, where I shall dwell in the light of Thy radiant Face.

Ant. LET NOT YOUR HEART BE TROUBLED, NEITHER LET IT BE AFRAID.

V. YOU HAVE MERITED THESE TRIALS BY YOUR INFIDELITIES; YET IT IS NOT VENGEANCE, BUT COMPASSION, THAT CHASTISES YOU.

R. Redemption is suffering love. To be united to Jesus Christ is to suffer with Him, and with Him to save souls.

V. The Sacred Heart is the place of my rest.

R. Here will I dwell, for I have chosen it.

Let us pray.

O Saviour Jesus, at the sight of Thy Holy Face so disfigured by sorrow, at the sight of Thy Sacred Heart so full of love, I cry out with St. Augustine: Write, I beseech Thee, O Lord, Thy wounds upon my heart, that I may read therein sorrow and love; sorrow to, endure every sorrow for Thee, and love to despise every love for Thee.

V. O Face so full of compassion, by the sacred blood streaming from Thee,

R. By Thy divine humiliations and Thy glorious martyrdom,

V. Be the Redeemer of sinners.

R. O Jesus, save the world.

V. We will grasp Thy bleeding cross and bear it on our hearts.

R. May the souls of the faithful departed through the mercy of God rest in peace.

FRIDAY

COMPLINE

V. His holy Name shall be our shield.
R. And His adorable Face shall be our fortress.
Glory be to the Father.
Hymn
Virgins holy, matrons lowly,
Gleaning in His fields of wheat,
Widows prayerful, mothers careful,
Children playing near His feet;
Doctors, teachers, hermits, preachers,
Pouring out their oil arid wine,

Meet before Thee to adore Thee,

Lamb of God, O Christ divine!

How they love Thee! And above thee

Cloudless in the sapphire blue,

And below Thee, they who know Thee

Sing their anthems loud and true.

Ever flowing, red and glowing,

Is the blood-stream from Thy side,

Feeding, laving, cheering, saving,

Holy Church Thy chosen bride.

E. H. M,

Dear Jesus, we offer Thee, in reparation for blasphemies, all the glory that the Blessed Virgin and St. Joseph, the holy angels and all the saints have given Thee, now give Thee, and will give Thee for all eternity.

And we offer Thee for all unbelieving words, whether spoken or written, the prayers and aspirations of religious, the zeal of, missionaries, the holy desires of souls consecrated to Thee in the world, the tears of those in affliction, the resignation of the poor, the humility of pure hearts, and the blood of martyrs.

Ant. THIS NEW HARMONY, THE PRAYER OF REPARATION, IS PLEASING TO MY EARS, REJOICES THE ANGELS, AND CALMS THE WRATH OF THE ETERNAL FATHER.

V. I WILL HIDE THEE IN MY HEART.

R. O sweet Jesus, let me never go out from that place of retreat. I abandon myself to Thee without will or self-seeking. Do with me what Thou wilt, only let me never he separated from Thee.

V. The Sacred Heart is the place of my rest.

R. Here will I dwell, for I have chosen it.

Let us pray.

O Saviour Jesus, at the sight of Thy Holy Face so disfigured by sorrow, at the sight of Thy Sacred Heart so full of love, I cry out with St. Augustine: Write, I beseech Thee, O Lord, Thy wounds upon my heart, that I may read therein sorrow and love; sorrow to, endure every sorrow for Thee, and love to despise every love for Thee.

V. O Face so full of compassion, by the sacred blood streaming from Thee,

R. By Thy divine humiliations and Thy glorious martyrdom,

V. Be the Redeemer of sinners.

R. O Jesus, save the world.

V. We will grasp Thy bleeding cross and bear it on our hearts.

R. May the souls of the faithful departed through the mercy of God rest in peace.

Prayer.

O Jesus, Thou art surely God to bear with us and dwell so patiently among us. How few there are who have the courage to range themselves under Thy standard and do battle with those who lead Thee again to Calvary!

As in the days of Thy passion. Thou art alone in the hands. of Thine enemies. Alas, if we have not the gift of tears like St. Peter, at least let us beat our breasts with the multitude returning to Jerusalem and acknowledging that "indeed this was the Son of God." O Holy Spirit, enliven us, and give us courage to throw ourselves in the vanguard of the strife. Give us the victory, and let all hearts own Thee for their king.

V. Adorable Jesus, teach us to compassionate Thy sufferings on earth, that we may merit to have a share in Thy glory in heaven.

R. This Face so marred and bruised shall one day appear, radiant in glory, and its enemies shall be annihilated forever.

V. The spirits of evil shall be driven back into darkness, and the Holy Face shall reign upon earth.

Blessed art thou, O Israel. Who is like unto thee, O people that art saved by the Lord, the shield of thy help, the sword of thy glory! Thine enemies shall deny thee and thou shalt tread upon their necks.

Lord, let us walk in the light of Thy Face, and rejoice day and night in the praise of Thy Name.

V. May the souls of the faithful departed through the mercy of God

rest in peace.

R. And may the chains be broken that hold them captive far from Thy

Face. Amen

SATURDAY

MATIN

Hail Mary.

O Jesus, Thou hast promised all good gifts to those who adore Thy Holy Face in reparation for blasphemies uttered against Thy holy Name and the teachings of Thy Church.

Offer to the eternal Father, we implore Thee, these prayers which we pour forth for the greater glory of God and the conversion of sinners.

Our Father who art in heaven, look not upon us only, but upon the Face of Thy Christ.

V. O Lord, show us Thy Face, and we shall be saved.

R. Turn Thy Face towards us, arid give us peace.

V. His mighty Name shall be our shield.

R. And His adorable Face shall be our fortress.

Glory be to the Father.

Hymn

First-crowned, most loved of all the brides elect,

My Mother Mary, on thy throne thou art;

And as I see thee through this twilight dim,

The still, calm splendor of thy glory grows

Brighter and brighter round me, and Thy love Deepens and widens.

Because of all our Father's gifts, thou art

The light of many worlds, the ocean-star,

The joy of saints victorious and crowned,

Lily of lilies in God's Paradise.

Rawes

Lord, Thy Heart is an inexhaustible fountain of love.

Thou didst keep nothing back. Thou hadst given all things for us, save only Thy holy and well-beloved Mother.

But the nations gathered around Thy cross form but one family, and a family must have a mother.

Jesus therefore gives us His most precious treasure, His blessed and immaculate Mother.

Mary, gazing on the bruised and bleeding Face of her Son, is inspired with generous love for these guilty creatures whom Jesus has given her for children.

Blessed be the compassion of Jesus, who will not leave us orphans.

Blessed be the tender heart of Mary, that longs for the salvation of the murderers of her Son.

Ant. GO TO MY MOTHER.

V. O most worthy Mother of Jesus, in thy hands I place the interests of the holy Name of Jesus.

148

R. Sweet heart of Mary, be my love; sweet Heart of Jesus, be my salvation.

V. Mercy goes before the Face of God.

R. And they who walk in the light of His Countenance shall enter into the joys of the Church triumphant.

Let us Pray

Holy Father, protect the Church of Jesus Christ for His holy Name's sake. This was the last will of Thine only-begotten Son. Forget not His prayer on that last night of His earthly life: "Holy Father, keep them in Thy Name whom Thou hast given Me; that they may be one, as We also are. While I was with them I kept them in Thy Name. Those whom Thou gavest Me I have kept. Sanctify them in truth. Thy word is truth." Hear us when we pray for Jesus' sake.

V. Unbelievers attack the majesty of God.

R. Lord, I invoke Thy mercy, and I bow before Thy justice.

V. May Thy holy Name be known and loved, world without end.

R. May the souls of the faithful departed, through the mercy of. God, rest in peace.

SATURDAY

LAUDS

V. His holy Name shall be our shield.

R. And His adorable Face shall be our fortress.

Glory be to the Father.

Hymn

And what Thou art to us, oh, who can say,

Thou Beacon of the storm-tossed mariner.

A sweet face looking on us in the dusk,

A heart that loves us with a changeless love;—

These things art thou, sweet Queen of light and love,

Dear star-crowned Mother, fairest and most blest.

Rawes

O gift inestimable, O legacy divine, O sacred inheritance of the Heart of Jesus, we receive Thee with tears of gratitude and love. Thou knowest, O God, the weakness of our poor humanity, the. temptations which attack us and agitate us as a reed is shaken by the wind; To sustain us in these trials and dangers, Thou hast given us Thine own Mother. With her we will fear nothing; with her we dare ask all and hope all.

Sweetest Mother, we consecrate ourselves to thy service, and we rest our weary heads on thy immaculate heart. Next to the Heart of Jesus, this is our refuge and our home.

Ant. SHE SHALL SPEAK TO ME FOR YOU.

V. Our Lady of the Holy Face, pray for us.

R. O most holy and helpful Virgin Mary, send forth a tide of grace and mercy on all who call themselves thy children.

V. Mercy shall go before the Face of God.

R. And they who walk in the light of His Face shall enter into the joys of the Church triumphant.

Let us pray.

Holy Father, protect the Church of Jesus Christ for His holy Name's sake. This was the last will of Thine only-begotten Son. Forget not His prayer on that last night of His earthly life: "Holy Father, keep them in Thy Name whom Thou hast given Me; that they may be one, as We also are. While I was with them I kept them in Thy Name. Those whom Thou gavest Me I have kept. Sanctify them in truth. Thy word is truth." Hear us when we pray for Jesus' sake.

V. Unbelievers attack the majesty of God.

R. Lord, I invoke Thy mercy, and I bow before Thy justice.

V. May Thy holy Name be known and loved, world without end.

R. May the souls of the faithful departed, through the mercy of God, rest in peace.

SATURDAY

PRIME

V. His holy Name shall be our shield.

R. And His adorable Face shall be our fortress.

Glory be to the Father.

Hymn

My child, the school of love is here,

The school that teacheth to endure.

The night is just begun.

Through awful shades, through sweat of blood,

Through every pain that tries the soul,

That crushes nerve and flesh, the Master leads.

There is no pang He beareth not, no grief He tasteth not.

Gethsemani

"And they gave Him gall and vinegar to drink" —fit emblem of the cruelty and malice of men.

"Charity hath failed." What have we done for the souls for whom He thirsted? Thou art thirsting for our hearts; the love of souls consumes Thee, O blessed Lord! We give Thee to drink of our love. Satisfy Thyself with this poor cup; this day we make a full oblation; we consecrate ourselves to Thee without reserve.

Ant. MY FATHER AND MY CHURCH ARE DESPISED AND OUTRAGED BY MY ENEMIES.

V. Will no one defend them?

R. Our Lord has promised that He will defend before the Father all who embrace this work of reparation, and by their written or spoken words, by by their prayers, defend His cause. He Himself will wipe all tears from their eyes, and the stains of sin from their souls.

V. Mercy goeth before the Face of God.

R. And they who walk in the light of His Countenance shall enter into the joys of the Church triumphant.

Let us pray.

Holy Father, protect the Church of Jesus Christ for His holy Name's sake. This was the last will of Thine only-begotten Son. Forget not His prayer on that last night of His earthly life: "Holy Father, keep them in Thy Name whom Thou hast given Me; that they may be one, as We also are. While I was with them I kept them in Thy Name. Those whom Thou gavest Me I have kept. Sanctify them in truth. Thy word is truth." Hear us when we pray for Jesus' sake.

V. Unbelievers attack the majesty of God.

R. Lord, I invoke Thy mercy, and I bow before Thy justice.

V. May Thy holy Name be known and loved, world without end.

R. May the souls of the faithful departed, through the mercy of God, rest in peace.

SATURDAY

TIERCE

V. His holy Name shall be our shield.

R. And His adorable Face shall be our fortress.

Glory be to the Father.

Hymn

He dieth as a King; He dieth as a God.

The crown of thorns He weareth to the end.

And bows His royal head as Prince of life and death.

Deeper, darker will the shadows grow,

The midnight horror yet shall come.

It shall be colder than the grave,

And every light but His shall die.

Gethsemani

"And Jesus, crying with a loud voice, gave up the ghost." A cry, of sorrow for souls; a cry of grief that they would not be saved; a cry of love and exultation in sacrifice; a pleading cry to souls rushing oh to their destruction.

And the earth trembled, arid the dead came out of their graves to proclaim the power of the Crucified. Men denied Him, but the rocks were rent, and all nature lifted up its voice to proclaim Him sovereign Lord.

O cleansing blood, thou criest for vengeance and for pardon; thou criest for the condemnation or the salvation of the world. Cry again, O Precious Blood; let the cry of victory sound in heaven and in regenerate hearts.',

Ant. THINK OF THE MULTITUDE OF SOULS TO WHOM THESE THOUGHTS NEVER COME!

V. WORK FOR YOURSELF AND FOR THEM; BE TO THEM AS A TENDER MOTHER, SHARING ALL SHE HAS WITH HER CHILDREN.

R. Whatsoever my hand findeth to do, I will do it with all my heart. Glorify Thyself in my weakness, and triumph over every obstacle which separates me from Thee.

V. Mercy shall go before the Face of God.

R. They who walk in the light of My Countenance shall enter into the joys of the Church triumphant.

Let us pray.

Holy Father, protect the Church of Jesus Christ for His holy Name's sake. This was the last will of Thine only-begotten Son. Forget not His prayer on that last night of His earthly life: "Holy Father, keep them in Thy Name whom Thou hast given Me; that they may be one, as We also are. While I was with them I kept them in Thy Name. Those whom Thou gavest Me I have kept. Sanctify them in truth. Thy word is truth." Hear us when we pray for Jesus' sake.

V. Unbelievers attack the majesty of God.

R. Lord, I invoke Thy mercy, and I bow before Thy justice.

V. May Thy holy Name be known and loved, world without end.

R. May the souls of the faithful departed, through the mercy of God, rest in peace.

SATURDAY

SEXT

V. His mighty Name shall be our shield.

R. And His adorable Face shall be our fortress.

Glory be to the Father.

Hymn

The child that seeks to keep his vigil here

Must bid farewell to all created things.

Must come to lie beneath the funeral pall,

Must come to seek a burial with the skulls.

Only Jesus here, and Jesus on His cross.

For I shall hide myself behind the clouds,

And in the unearthly gloom shall only point to Him.

Gethsemani

V. Jesus is dead. I adore in silence I gaze upon His dead Face, and my soul is filled with its serenity and peace.

Lord, I will abide close to Thy heart. Thy Face shall be the pillar of light to guide me amid the shadows of earth. Thy cross shall be my pilgrim's staff, Thy open side shall be my haven of rest, the warm shelter from the coldness of the world that loves Thee not. And one day, when my poor soul has been purified by suffering, O dear Face of my Saviour, Thou wilt come, and in a last and ineffable Communion Thou wilt give it the kiss of eternal love.

R. Eternal Father, look upon the heart, the soul, the divinity of Jesus; look upon Him who hath loved us and given Himself a sacrifice for us.

V. Mercy shall go before the Face of God.

R. They who walk in the light of My Countenance shall enter into the joys of the Church triumphant.

Let us pray.

Holy Father, protect the Church of Jesus Christ for His holy Name's sake. This was the last will of Thine only-begotten Son. Forget not His prayer on that last night of His earthly life: "Holy Father, keep them in Thy Name whom Thou hast given Me; that they may be one, as We also are. While I was with them I kept them in Thy Name. Those whom Thou gavest Me I have kept. Sanctify them in truth. Thy word is truth." Hear us when we pray for Jesus' sake.

V. Unbelievers attack the majesty of God.

R. Lord, I invoke Thy mercy, and I bow before Thy justice.

V. May Thy holy Name be known and loved, world without end.

R. May the souls of the faithful departed, through the mercy of God, rest in peace.

Saturday

None

V. His holy Name shall be our shield.

R. And His adorable Face shall be our fortress.

Glory be to the Father.

Hymn

Behold, my child, thy Bridegroom and thy King.

This is indeed the place of death; here all of earth must die.

That death is sweet.

The icy grave is portal to the palace of thy Spouse.

The wounded hands are waiting for thy last caress.

The mangled feet will lead thee to thy home.

The bruised and bleeding Face will smile When thou art dead to all but

Him,

The precious lips are yearning

For thy loving kiss.

There are still some drops of blood within the Sacred Heart of Jesus crucified, and it must all be shed.

Those who pierce the loving heart of Jesus and cause the Precious Blood to flow afresh, shall feel the healing power of this saving flood.

Within this open wound I place all who are dear to me, that we may be united in this divine sanctuary.

There I place all my enemies, and Thine, O blessed Saviour. There, too, I place Thy Church, wearing the purple mantle of scorn and the crown of thorns.

When humiliation or crucifixion comes to me, I will say, This is the voice of love, calling me to sacrifice with Jesus. Let me go to the open wound of His side, and draw from thence, as from a fountain, strength and courage to endure with patience.

Ant. HONOR THE HEART OF MY MOTHER WITH MINE. LET THEM NEVER BE SEPARATED.

V. PRAY FOR YOURSELF AND FOR SINNERS. THEN WILL I FORGET YOUR PAST INGRATITUDES.

R. The cross of Christ planted on the Rock of Peter is our firm anchor of hope.

V. Mercy goes before the Face of God.

R. They who walk in the light of My Face shall enter into the joys of the Church triumphant.

Let us pray.

Holy Father, protect the Church of Jesus Christ for His holy Name's sake. This was the last will of Thine only-begotten Son. Forget not His prayer on that last night of His earthly life: "Holy Father, keep them in Thy Name whom Thou hast given Me; that they may be one, as We also are. While I was with them I kept them in Thy Name. Those whom Thou gavest Me I have kept. Sanctify them in truth. Thy word is truth." Hear us when we pray for Jesus' sake.

V. Unbelievers attack the majesty of God.

R. Lord, I invoke Thy mercy, and I bow before Thy justice.

V. May Thy holy Name be known and loved, world without end.

R. May the souls of the faithful departed, through the mercy of God, rest in peace.

SATURDAY

VESPERS

V. His holy Name shall be our shield.

R. And His adorable Face shall be our fortress.

Glory be to the Father.

Hymn

The Queen of sorrows rules on Calvary;

You could not move without her help.

No soul can watch upon the mountain drear,

Unless she hold him in her mantle pure,

And hold his hands amid the phantoms of the grave

Where Jesus lies.

Gethsemani

O tender Mother, thy tears reproach me. With mournful eyes thou dost count the wounds of thy divine Son as He lies lifeless within thine arms. We have killed the Son, and have broken the heart of the Mother. That flesh which thou didst give Him, He took for love of us. The. blood He took from thee, He shed it all for us. O Mary, our tears mingle with thine. While life lasts we will expiate those sins which caused the death of our Saviour and wounded thy maternal heart.

Ant. RETURN UNTO THY FATHER'S HOUSE, WHICH IS NONE OTHER THAN HIS HEART.

V. I AM ALL-POWERFUL, AND I WILL SUFFER NONE TO SNATCH THEE FROM MY BOSOM.

R. Most holy and immaculate Virgin, I implore thee to offer to God the Precious Blood of thy beloved Son Jesus, for grace to hinder one mortal sin, somewhere in the world this day.

V. Mercy shall go before the Face of God.

R. They who walk in the light of My Face shall enter into the joys of the Church triumphant.

Let us pray.

Holy Father, protect the Church of Jesus Christ for His holy Name's sake. This was the last will of Thine only-begotten Son. Forget not His prayer on that last night of His earthly life: "Holy Father, keep them in Thy Name whom Thou hast given Me; that they may be one, as We also are. While I was with them I kept them in Thy Name. Those whom Thou gavest Me I have kept. Sanctify them in truth. Thy word is truth." Hear us when we pray for Jesus' sake.

V. Unbelievers attack the majesty of God.

R. Lord, I invoke Thy mercy, and I bow before Thy justice.

V. May Thy holy Name be known and loved, world without end.

R. May the souls of the faithful departed, through the mercy of God, rest in peace.

SATURDAY

COMPLINE

V. His holy Name shall be our shield.

R. And His adorable Face shall be our fortress.

Glory be to the Father.

Hymn

As on they journey to the close,

These wounded feet and mine,

Distincter still the vision grows,

And more and more divine,—

For in my Guide's wide-open side

The riven heart I see,

And the tender voice sobs like a psalm,

"This Heart was pierced for thee!"

For me, great God! for me?

"Yea, enter in, my love, my lamb,

This Heart was pierced for thee!"

E. C. Donnelly

The tomb has hidden the Holy Face of the Sun of justice, but death cannot hold Him Who is the source, of life. We are close bound within the tomb of our iniquities, the hardness of our hearts is the stone that separates us from Him. Lord, roll away the stone and snatch us from death eternal. Break down the hateful wall that hides Thy glorious Face.

Face of my risen Jesus, have pity on all desolate souls, all lost and abandoned souls. Let the clouds that rest upon our darkened hearts vanish before the radiance of Thy Face. Let the whole world know Thee, and sing the: praises of the victories of the love of Jesus.

Ant. I HAVE REVEALED TO THEE THIS WORK OF REPARATION; I HAVE SHOWN THEE ITS BEAUTY, AND NOW I PROMISE THEE THE REWARD.

V. I die of thirst to behold the adorable Face of my Lord Jesus.[1] Mercy shall go before the Face of God.

R. They who walk in the light of My Face shall enter into the joys of the Church triumphant.

Let us pray.

Holy Father, protect the Church of Jesus Christ for His holy Name's sake. This was the last will of Thine only-begotten Son. Forget not His prayer on that last night of His earthly life: "Holy Father, keep them in Thy Name whom Thou hast given Me; that they may be one, as We also are. While I was with them I kept them in Thy Name. Those

---

1. Last words of M. Dupont.

whom Thou gavest Me I have kept. Sanctify them in truth. Thy word is truth." Hear us when we pray for Jesus' sake.

V. Unbelievers attack the majesty of God.

R. Lord, I invoke Thy mercy, and I bow before Thy justice.

V. May Thy holy Name be known and loved, world without end.

R. May the souls of the faithful departed, through the mercy of God, rest in peace.

Prayer.

O Jesus, Thou art surely God to bear with us and dwell so patiently among us. How few there are who have the courage to range themselves under Thy standard and do battle with those who lead Thee again to Calvary!

As in the days of Thy passion. Thou art alone in the hands. of Thine enemies. Alas, if we have not the gift of tears like St. Peter, at least let us beat our breasts with the multitude returning to Jerusalem and acknowledging that "indeed this was the Son of God." O Holy Spirit, enliven us, and give us courage to throw ourselves in the vanguard of the strife. Give us the victory, and let all hearts own Thee for their king.

V. Adorable Jesus, teach us to compassionate Thy sufferings on earth, that we may merit to have a share in Thy glory in heaven.

R. This Face so marred and bruised shall one day appear, radiant in glory, and its enemies shall be annihilated forever.

V. The spirits of evil shall be driven back into darkness, and the Holy Face shall reign upon earth.

Blessed art thou, O Israel. Who is like unto thee, O people that art saved by the Lord, the shield of thy help, the sword of thy glory! Thine enemies shall deny thee and thou shalt tread upon their necks.

Lord, let us walk in the light of Thy Face, and rejoice day and night in the praise of Thy Name.

V. May the souls of the faithful departed through the mercy of God

rest in peace.

R. And may the chains be broken that hold them captive far from Thy

Face. Amen.